LANCELOT

or

THE KNIGHT OF THE CART

LANCELOT

or

THE KNIGHT
OF THE CART

Chrétien de Troyes

Translated by
Ruth Harwood Cline

THE UNIVERSITY OF GEORGIA PRESS
Athens and London

© 1990 by the University of Georgia Press
Athens, Georgia 30602
www.ugapress.org
All rights reserved

Set in 11 on 13 Linotron Bembo

Printed digitally in the United States of America

Library of Congress Cataloging-in-Publication Data

Chrétien, de Troyes, 12th cent.
[Chevalier de la charrette. English]
Lancelot, or, The knight of the cart / Chrétien de Troyes ;
translated by Ruth Harwood Cline.
xxxiv, 231 p. ; 24 cm.
Translation of: Chevalier de la charrette.
Includes bibliographical references (p. 197–231).
ISBN 0-8203-1212-6 (alk. paper)
ISBN 0-8203-1213-4 (pbk. : alk. paper)
1. Lancelot (Legendary character)—Romances.   2. Knights
and knighthood—Poetry.   3. Arthurian romances.
I. Cline, Ruth Harwood.   II. Title.
PQ1445.L3E5 1990
841'.1—dc20
89-20283
CIP

Paperback ISBN-13: 978-0-8203-1213-2

British Library Cataloging-in-Publication Data available

CONTENTS

ACKNOWLEDGMENTS

The genesis of this translation was an excursion to the Forest of Paimpont or Brocéliande and the Fountain of Barenton in 1984, when I was pondering how to respond to encouragement from some other members of the International Arthurian Society to prepare another translation of Chrétien. During that summer hike, I realized that the forest and fountain were exactly as Chrétien had described them in *Yvain*. The forest was thick and deep, its sandy, dusty paths were edged with clumps of thorn and briar, and a small path led to the place where the occasional bird sang in a great pine overshadowing the stone and fountain. Since the Fountain of Barenton is a peat spring, gaseous bubbles continuously boiled to the surface of the clear cold water. Of course there were no jewels, and water poured on the stone was followed hours later by a mild shower that did not alleviate the Breton draught. Yet I was greatly impressed by the accuracy of the details of Chrétien's twelfth-century description of the site, as perceptive and timeless as his insights into human nature, and I decided to make the commitment of time and translate *Lancelot*.

I am very grateful to others who took time from crowded professional and personal schedules to assist me in bringing this translation to completion. I thank William Roach for his encouragement and guidance in the resolution of textual variants and ambiguous vocabulary. I am deeply indebted to JoAnn Moran of Georgetown University for her timely assistance with the introduction, particularly for bringing her expertise as a medieval historian to the sections on the historical and literary Arthur and courtly love. I am tremendously grateful to Joan Tasker Grimbert of Catholic University for the scrupulous attention she gave to the entire manuscript and for her valuable insights into its nuances and final form. Of course, the responsibility for any errors is exclusively my own.

As ever, I thank my husband, William R. Cline, for his interest and assistance. This translation is dedicated to my daughters: Alison Margaret Cline and Marian Harwood Cline.

RUTH HARWOOD CLINE

[vii]

INTRODUCTION

Writing an introduction to a romance by Chrétien de Troyes is always challenging. Virtually nothing is known about the poet's life. Yet he dominates French literature of the twelfth century as Shakespeare did English literature of the sixteenth century. Chrétien was a writer of genius who drew upon various materials: Celtic tales and legends, classical myths, Christian themes, early histories of Britain, and the love songs of the troubadours, and created major works of literature with vivid characters and well-constructed plots whose influence has radiated over the centuries. A comprehensive study of his works requires the space of a library, not an introduction, and virtually no statement can be made about his romances without arousing intense and informed scholarly debate. Yet many English readers are unfamiliar with Chrétien's Old French works. They are more likely to have read Chrétien's fifteenth-century English successor Malory and are unable to situate Chrétien in the traditions of the twelfth-century courts over which Eleanor of Aquitaine and her daughter Marie of Champagne presided in France. Some genuinely believe that Chrétien's Arthurian romances describe a united kingdom of Britain, ruled by King Arthur and Queen Guinevere in turreted Camelot, that surely must have existed in history because it has existed so long in literature.

Chrétien's romance of Lancelot and Guinevere seems the place to discuss the historical and literary Arthur because of this character's position as the husband of the heroine. It is also the place to note that before Chrétien wrote this romance there was no known story of Lancelot and Guinevere, no reference in history or literature to a love affair between this knight and Arthur's wife. There were earlier stories of unfaithful queens; the best known was about Queen Iseut and her love for Tristan. There was an early account of an abduction of Guinevere and her rescue by Arthur, and another reference in a fanciful history to Guinevere's adultery with Mordred, which precipitated the last battle in which Arthur fell. But Chrétien de Troyes created the earliest romance of Lancelot and Guinevere; the names of these famous lovers were first linked in this twelfth-century story of the knight of the cart. Moreover, he handled the story according to the literary conventions of what is imprecisely known as courtly love, in which the knight's passion is expressed by adoration of the lady and submission to her will. The importance of *Lancelot* in literature cannot be exaggerated; it is comparable only to Chrétien's last romance, the earliest version of the story of the grail.

Therefore, while far more could be said about the sources, interpretations, and influence of this romance than is possible in this limited space, the introduction is intended to ensure the new reader an informed reading of the text and to guide the interested reader to the many comprehensive studies of Chrétien's works.

The Life and Works of Chrétien de Troyes

Biographical information about Chrétien de Troyes is based more on deduction and conjecture than on fact, but the poet is thought to have been born at Troyes in Champagne around 1135.[1] Troyes was a major trade center with an important annual fair and the seat of the counts of Champagne.[2] Count Henry of Champagne was closely allied with the royal house of France, and his wife Marie became Chrétien's literary patron.[3] Chrétien apparently received a classical education as part of his clerical training and began his literary career by composing verse adaptations of Ovid's *Art of Love* and *Remedy for Love*, two tales from the *Metamorphoses*, "The Shoulder Bite" and "Philomena," two love songs, and a tale of King Mark and Queen Iseut. With the exception of the love songs and "Philomena," these early works were lost.[4] His surviving works mostly focus on tales of Arthur and other Celtic fifth- or sixth-century heroes of Britain, tales that had been transmitted to France through Brittany and were part of the repertory of the minstrels who entertained the twelfth-century nobility.[5] Chrétien was the first writer to use the long *romanz* form of narrative verse in rhymed octosyllabic couplets in the vernacular to incorporate these tales into carefully crafted stories of the loves and adventures of prominent knights of Arthur's court, thus creating the Arthurian romance as a literary genre.[6] Of the works attributed with certainty to Chrétien, between 1160 and 1170 he wrote the first known Arthurian romance, *Erec and Enide,* signing it "Chrétien of Troyes," which implies that he was not living in Troyes at that time.[7] He returned to Troyes, presumably after 1164, an accepted date of the marriage of Marie Capet, the elder daughter of Eleanor of Aquitaine and King Louis VII of France, to Henry (the Liberal), count of Champagne, the brother of Louis VII's third wife Adele. *Erec and Enide* was followed by *Cligés,* written around 1176; and *Lancelot; or, The Knight of the Cart* and *Yvain; or, The Knight with the Lion,* both written between 1177 and 1181 (see note 36). In 1181 Count Henry of Champagne returned from the Holy Land and died, and Countess Marie retired from public life. Chrétien wrote his final work: *Perceval; or, The Story of the Grail,* under the patronage of Philip of Alsace, count of Flanders, regent of France during the minority of Louis VII's young son Philip-Augustus by his wife Adele. Chrétien's authorship of another romance, *William of England,* is disputed. Chrétien died sometime after 1190, leaving *Perceval* unfinished.

Arthur in History

The historical Arthur who inspired the Celtic tales that resulted six centuries later in these romances is an elusive figure who may not ever have existed.[8] As Rome declined, the Romanized Celts in Britain (Britons) who inhabited the outermost province of the Empire were directed to defend themselves, for they could no longer look to Rome for protection against savage Saxon and Pictish invaders. The date for the withdrawal of the Roman army from Britain is traditionally thought to be A.D. 410. There are no records of historical incidents in Britain for several centuries after that date that meet contemporary standards of accuracy.[9] Gradually the Britons reverted to their earlier political structure of small kingships, and the balance of power shifted against them as the barbarians moved westward. By the end of the sixth century the Saxons had moved so far west that many Britons migrated to Brittany and Galicia.[10]

At some early point when the Britons were threatened by a revolt of the Saxons in Britain, with land-taking aided by the Picts,

Saxon allies from the north, it is generally believed that a war leader emerged who bore the Welsh version of the Roman name Artorius and led a significant resistance movement culminating in an important victory against the barbarians at Mount Badon around 518.[11] There is no historical evidence that this Arthur was a king, and, while certain places, particularly in the West Country, are associated with him, the modern image of Camelot bears little resemblance to these Roman cities and Celtic strongholds.[12] Whoever the leader of the defense of Britain may have been, the Saxons were temporarily confined to the territory of Canterbury and Kent.[13] When the leader fell, allegedly at the Battle of Camlann in 539, the Saxons moved westward, overwhelmed the Britons, and became the dominant group in the British population until the Norman conquest in 1066.[14]

Arthur and Guinevere in Literature

The renown of Arthur is derived, not from his real life, but from his real role in legend, myth, and literature.[15] The vanquished Britons had every reason to cherish Arthur's memory and preserve it in tales and legends handed down through the centuries of Saxon domination.[16] Early in the twelfth century, the Normans, established on the British throne by conquest after their victory over the Saxons in 1066, welcomed literary works that supported their position by describing the brutal Saxon conquest of the Britons in the sixth century and the Britons' valiant struggle to deter them. Thus works about Arthur appeared early in the twelfth century, such as William of Malmesbury's *Acts of the Kings of England* in 1125, Caradoc of Llancarfan's *Life of St. Gildas* in 1130, and Geoffrey of Monmouth's *History of the Kings of Britain* in 1136. These works became important source material for Chrétien's romances.[17]

Geoffrey of Monmouth, who was Welsh or born of Breton parents in Wales, wrote a *History of the Kings of Britain* that, although mostly fanciful, was exceedingly influential. Geoffrey traces the settlement and kings of Britain from the Trojan Aeneas' great-grandson Brutus through the rise and fall of Rome. He describes how the Breton prince Constantine became king and was ultimately succeeded by his younger sons Aurelius Ambrosius and Uther Pendragon, the father of Arthur, after the usurper Vortigern allowed the Saxons to settle in Britain and ravage the country. The *History* contains a comprehensive account of Arthur's ascent to power—of his twelve battles with the Saxons, ending with victory on Mount Badon in 516—as he fought under the sign of the cross, and then of his European conquests. At Rome Arthur learned that his sister's son Mordred had bigamously married Queen Guinevere and staged a coup from their headquarters at London Tower. Arthur returned for the last Battle of Camlann in 542, where he slew Mordred but was mortally wounded himself, and Guinevere, contrite, retired to a convent.[18] Geoffrey's *History,* a Latin prose work, was translated and adapted into French verse in 1155 by Wace, who greatly expanded the portion on Arthur, and Chrétien de Troyes was familiar with it.[19]

Celtic Influence in *Lancelot*

Other Celtic tales that are reflected in *Lancelot* became known in France, many stories of knights who visited the Otherworld, a fourth-dimensional realm outside of conventional time and space, or who had encounters with fairy beings.[20] There was a genre of *aitheda,* or elopement tales, reflecting tribal raids among the Irish for women and property.[21] Many involved the abduction of the wife of a ruler and her visit to the Otherworld, heralded by hospitable hosts and perilous passages, culminating in her rescue by her husband and his men.[22] In some the wife herself was a fairy who had married a mortal, until she was ultimately claimed by her fairy husband and returned to his realm.[23] Such an abduction tale was told about Guinevere in the *Life of St. Gildas* by Caradoc of Llancarfan, written around 1130. Melwas, the King of Somerset, abducted Arthur's wife Guennuvar and took her to Glastonbury, which was surrounded by water. Arthur raised an army from Devon and Cornwall and came to rescue her. After mediation by Gildas and the abbot of Glastonbury, the queen was returned.[24] A version of this abduction tale is depicted in stone on the cathedral in Modena, but Lancelot is not mentioned in these sources.[25]

The most famous Celtic story that involved a dispute between a king and lover over the king's wife was that of the half-savage, half-civilized love affair of Queen Iseut and Tristan, the wife and nephew of King Mark of Cornwall. By the twelfth century the Tristan legend was renowned in various forms. Some were more refined and told how a love potion, intended to create eternal love between King Mark and Iseut, is inadvertently consumed by Iseut and Tristan on the voyage from Ireland to Cornwall and thus dooms a loyal pair to an irresistible passion that leads them to betray a noble king. Other versions deemphasized the love potion and described an ardent and conniving pair deliberately outwitting a jealous and cruel husband. Béroul's version is closer to the primitive legend: the potion wanes but the lovers continue to repent and relapse into their passion. What many critics consider the more courtly version, written by Thomas d'Angleterre around 1175 (possibly for Eleanor of Aquitaine), focuses on the love relationship between Tristan and Iseut, of which the potion is symbolic rather than creative.[26]

Courtly Love

These Celtic tales of Arthur and other heroes and the subject of love were popular at two of the brightest courts in Europe: that of Eleanor of Aquitaine in Poitiers and of her daughter Countess Marie of Champagne in Troyes.[27] Marie Capet was born in 1145 and betrothed in childhood (1158) to Count Henry of Champagne, whom she married in 1164 when he was nearly twice her age. A cultivated princess, conservatively reared in a religious court by two stepmothers, Countess Marie presided over literary gatherings where for recreation the aristocracy listened to the love songs and lyric poetry of the troubadours, possibly submitted problems of the heart for discussion and judgment in the "courts of love," and were entertained by recitations of the fashionable Celtic tales of King Arthur and his knights in the repertory of the minstrels. It is quite possible that, under the patronage of Eleanor, Geoffrey of Monmouth wrote his *History of the Kings of England*, Wace his *Roman de Brut*, and Thomas d'Angleterre his *Tristan*; the troubadour Bernart de Ventadorn sang her praises in impassioned lyrics. Under the patronage of Countess Marie, Chrétien wrote his *Lancelot* and possibly his other three Arthurian romances.[28]

Gaston Paris coined the term "courtly love" in 1883 to describe the type of love that was celebrated in Provencal love lyrics and discussed in the twelfth-century courts. This literary convention began to emerge as early as 1102 in the sensual and consensual love poems of Eleanor's grandfather, William IX, duke of Aquitaine. Courtly love had certain roots in Ovid, who had written cynically about love and its cure in Roman times, and certain Arabic roots in the love poetry of Andalusia about the worship of the lady.[29] Although each troubadour sang of his individual experience, courtly love developed in two general trends: in the Southern interpretation the lady's role tended to be more erotic and adulterous, and in the Northern interpretation her role tended to be more chaste and remote. But in its refinement courtly love was the antithesis both of commonplace lust and of the destructive passion portrayed in the Tristan legend.

Courtly love was an ennobling and inspirational emotion felt by a lover, initially a troubadour but often later a knight, for a lady, sometimes the wife of a great and powerful nobleman.[30] In the genre of poems reflected in *Lancelot,* the lady herself was a figure of power, acting for her husband in his absence and presiding over a court that included aspiring knights and noble younger sons with little property. Its exaltation of the lady reflected her social distance from the knight; the courtly lover identified with the troubadour as he praised and adored the lady from afar for her great beauty and embodiment of all virtues and graces. Although denied nobility of rank, the lover achieved a nobility of spirit, for the lady's love, when won, increased his worth and enriched him.[31]

The treatment of courtly love evolved as it was sung by the troubadours, and the gifted ones were not wandering minstrels but stably attached to noble courts. One of the earlier troubadours, Marcabru, who was supported by William X, duke of Aquitaine in the 1130s, linked courtly love, which unifies physical and mental desire and spiritual aspiration, with all courtly virtues, including moderation, reason, and the ability to discern good from bad, truth from falsehood, and to choose the right or straight path in life. Courtly love flowered in 1150 in the troubadour Bernart de Ventadorn's lyric celebration of the beauty of Queen Eleanor. Bernart held that courtly love required total devotion and submission to the noble lady (*domna*) and her idealized beauty and virtues; rejecting Marcabru's rationality, he praised the irrational joy and oblivion found in contemplation of the loved one.[32]

Both Marcabru and Bernart influenced Chrétien's treatment of Lancelot's love for the queen. The supremacy of the lady celebrated in lyrics of courtly love was expressed in accepted forms of behavior. Toward her lover the lady was described as being aloof and domineering, insistent upon secrecy, and demanding unfailing proof of great prowess, unswerving devotion, and absolute obedience. Only after he had passed her harsh tests of his worthiness and fidelity might she reward him by a token of her favor. The lover in turn was inspired to the greatest feats of prowess to impress her and to abject compliance with her every caprice. However valiant he might be in battle, in her presence he turned pale and trembled. In the quest of her favor he was prone to spells of rapt adoration of her person and fits of despondency at her cruelty. By Chrétien's time such behavior was a well-established literary convention.

At the courts of Champagne and Poitiers, much energy was expended on the dilemma of reconciling the knight's adoration of the lady with his obligations to society and the lady's conflicting allegiances to her courtly lover and husband. This relationship existed apart from the marital obligations of lover and lady. In the traditions of the South, the expectations of love's reward were more sensual; in the stricter North, the lady's tokens of favor were usually limited to a scarf, sleeve, or ribbon, a kiss, or an embrace.[33] While some love lyrics allude to physical consummation, sexual pleasure between lady and lover was also thwarted by gossips and spies even in the literary realm, and in reality the reprisals taken by jealous husbands were swift and severe. Thus courtly love tended to be a fantasy of adultery, a diversion of the leisure classes that probably did not distract them from practical considerations in marriage.[34]

The subject had reached the point of codification and possibly satire by 1185 in Andreas Capellanus' *The Art of Courtly Love*. Andreas described possibly fictitious "courts of love" to which problems of the heart were submitted to Eleanor or Countess Marie for their verdicts and prepared a list of "rules of love." Two of the most famous rules allegedly reflected Countess Marie's views that marriage was no impediment to courtly love, but courtly love could not exist in marriage.[35] While the knight Lancelot's devotion to the queen is the epitome of courtly love, the development of the grail legend that arose from Chrétien's final romance, *Perceval; or, The Story of the Grail,* composed after 1181, reflects a gradual displacement of the chivalric ideal, and in the literature of the later centuries the inspirational force behind great deeds of chivalry became not the love of the lady but the love of God.

Thus the aristocracy gathered at the courts of Poitiers and Champagne was sufficiently realistic to recognize that the relationship between courtly lover and lady was the antithesis of the relationship of Christian marriage, in which the wife was subservient to her husband in all matters and adultery a cardinal sin. For in its exaltation of the lady courtly love was a reversal of the actual position of women in the medieval hierarchy of church and state. Yet, in an era when marriages were arranged on the basis of property or dynastic considerations and were indissoluble, the contemplation of such a relationship had a certain appeal. Around 1177 Countess Marie, then in her early thirties and the mother of two children, specifically requested her court poet Chrétien to write a romance of courtly love based on the Celtic tales of the abduction and adultery of Queen Guinevere and to make the knight Lancelot her rescuer and lover.

Chrétien de Troyes was a clerk, probably in minor religious orders. In his two earlier romances, *Erec and Enide* and *Cligés,* and in *Yvain,* written concurrently with *Lancelot,* he endeavors to reconcile courtly love with marriage.[36] In his last romance, *Perceval,* the unmarried hero's love for the maiden Blancheflor is not developed fully, as the quest of the grail displaces the lady as a motivating force, but no impediment to their future marriage exists. Thus, while it is unlikely that the Countess's request for a literary portrayal of courtly love outside marriage shocked Chrétien, who was thoroughly familiar with the works of Ovid, the Tristan legend, and the lyrics of the troubadours, the adulterous nature of the romance may not have been entirely to his individual taste and may account for his decision not to finish it personally.

With the disclaimer in the flattering prologue that he was applying thought and effort to this work at Countess Marie's specific request and with instructions from her about how the material she had provided should be handled, Chrétien began the romance of *Lancelot; or, The Knight of the Cart,* the earliest known version of the celebrated love affair between Lancelot and Guinevere.

Summary

Lancelot begins at King Arthur's court at Camelot on the feast of the Ascension, when Meleagant, the brash young son of the King of Gorre, arrives suddenly and challenges the court by announcing that he has many of Arthur's subjects from Logres imprisoned in his land and that Arthur is powerless to do anything about it. Arthur agrees this is the case. Meleagant inquires whether Arthur has one knight so valiant that he would entrust the queen to his protection, in order to escort her to a nearby wood and defend her against Meleagant. If the knight successfully defends the queen, Meleagant will release the prisoners. The steward Kay announces his departure from court, and the king, unable to dissuade him, orders the queen to plead with him to stay and even fall down at his feet. Queen Guinevere obeys, and Kay requests an unknown boon, which the king and queen rashly grant. The boon is to accept Meleagant's challenge. Although Kay is not noted for valor, Arthur acquiesces, and no one else at court is much concerned about Guinevere's safety. As she mounts her palfrey to follow Kay, the queen murmurs about an unknown knight who would protect her if he were present.

Gawain galvanizes Arthur into action, and the court rides after the queen and finds Kay's riderless horse. A knight, who will not be named until midway through the romance, makes a dramatic appearance riding his horse to death. The knight, Lancelot, one of Gawain's closest friends, takes the nearer of Gawain's two steeds and rides off. When Gawain overtakes him, the second horse is dead at a scene of combat between Lancelot and several opponents, and the knight, walking determinedly on foot, has just overtaken a cart.

The cart is used to transport criminals to their punishment, and a man who has been carted forfeits all his feudal rights and lives his lifetime in disgrace. The dwarf driver promises Lancelot news of the queen if he will abase himself by riding in the cart, and after hesitating two steps the knight mounts the cart. Gawain refuses to mount the cart but rides alongside. Lancelot is humiliated by the townspeople and by the chatelaine of the castle where the two knights lodge that first night. He sleeps in the castle's Wondrous Bed and survives a midnight assault by a flaming lance. Next morning he catches a glimpse of Meleagant's party, with Kay on a litter and Guinevere being led away, and nearly yields to a sudden impulse to commit suicide.

Gawain and Lancelot meet a maiden at a crossroads, who tells them the way to Gorre in exchange for pledges. She names the abductor, Meleagant, and describes the land of Gorre as an Otherworld realm filled with prisoners and accessible by a Sword Bridge and a Water Bridge. The knights part; Gawain chooses the less dangerous Water Bridge, but Lancelot, who is committed to following the most direct way to the queen, undertakes to proceed toward the painful Sword Bridge.

Alone, lost in reverie about the queen, Lancelot is challenged by the guardian of a ford, who throws him into cold water. Lancelot defeats the guardian, whose maiden offers herself in exchange for the release of her lover. Faithful to Guinevere, Lancelot declines the offer but releases the guardian.

Seeking lodging the second night, Lancelot meets the fourth maiden, a sexual temptress who demands his presence in her bed in exchange for her hospitality. He reluctantly consents, but is not tempted even by a feigned rape scene the maiden has staged with her servants. When he shares her bed but turns his back on her, the maiden realizes the extraordinary nature of his quest and retires to her own room.

Next morning this lustful maiden asks Lancelot to allow her to accompany him according to the old custom of Logres and defend her against all abductors. As they pass a fountain he spots a beautiful comb with golden hairs and swoons when the maiden tells him that the comb and hair are Guinevere's. On a narrow path Lancelot is challenged by a suitor whom the maiden dislikes, and they proceed to a meadow where people are frolicking. The games are stopped to humiliate the cart knight, but the suitor's father forbids his son to fight with him. Father and son decide, however, to pursue him.

At a monastery Lancelot makes his only deviation from the straight way to Guinevere by stopping to pray. A monk shows him the cemetery and tombs, which are inscribed with the names of Arthur's most famous living knights. One tomb is for the liberator of the prisoners held in Gorre, and seven men are required to lift the heavy slab. Lancelot raises the slab alone, establishing himself as the liberator who will one day lie in that tomb. Abashed, the father, son, and temptress go away.

Crossing the border into Gorre, Lancelot accepts lodging the third night with a vavasor and his large family who are prisoners from Logres. They tell him about the stone passageway that lies ahead, and accompanied by two of the vavasor's sons, Lancelot triumphs over its guardian.

Lancelot initially accepts lodging for the fourth night with a man who lives far off, and then word comes that the liberator is in the land and the prisoners have rioted. Lancelot and his two companions follow this native of Gorre into a castle but are caught between two sliding doors. After Lancelot uses his fairy ring to verify that no spells are involved, his party escapes through the postern gate to join the fray on the side of Logres. He is acclaimed a hero, and everyone wants to offer him comfortable lodgings, but on this fourth night he stays with the family of a knight whose house is directly on his way.

Lancelot and his two companions spend the following day riding from dawn until evening without adventure and accept the hospitality of a second vavasor from Logres for the fifth night. At dinner a challenger appears and insults Lancelot for riding in the cart. Lancelot defeats this proud knight and offers to release him on the condition that he mount the cart. As the challenger refuses, a maiden arrives on a mule and requests the knight's head. Torn by the conflicting demands of mercy and generosity, Lancelot resolves the dilemma by evoking his personal policy of pardoning once but never twice. He offers to fight the challenger again and defeats and beheads him. He resumes his dinner, spends the night, and arrives on the sixth day at the Sword Bridge.

The Sword Bridge is a sharp blade two lances long that leads to

King Bademagu's castle, where Guinevere is confined. In addition to its formidable edge it seems to be guarded by two lions or leopards who lie in wait to devour the hero on the other side. Lancelot crosses it on bare hands and feet but discovers that the lions or leopards are a mirage. King Bademagu, far from pleased that his son has abducted the wife of a neighboring king, welcomes Lancelot and reassures him that Guinevere and he have made mutual arrangements so that she is constantly protected against Meleagant.[37]

Unable to persuade Meleagant to make peace or Lancelot to postpone the combat for Guinevere until his wounds have healed, Bademagu arranges for the duel to take place the next day. When Lancelot begins to lose ground because of his injuries, a maiden asks the queen to identify her unknown rescuer and then calls his name to urge him on. Afraid that his son may be killed, Bademagu asks the queen to stop Lancelot, and the parties agree that the combat for the queen will be held at Arthur's court one year from the day that Meleagant comes there to challenge Lancelot. When Lancelot is brought into the queen's presence, she astounds both Bademagu and him by refusing to speak with him and haughtily withdraws. Lancelot visits Kay, whose wounds have not healed despite Bademagu's treatment because Meleagant has his men apply poisoned dressings.

The queen refuses to leave Gorre without Gawain, and Lancelot goes to find him. He is captured by citizens of Gorre who do not realize he has safe-conduct, and the rumor of his death reaches the queen. The queen repents of her capricious conduct toward Lancelot and grieves and fasts until the rumor of her death reaches Lancelot. He attempts to commit suicide but is rescued. Back at the castle, Lancelot is joyfully received by Bademagu and graciously welcomed by the queen, and the lovers secretly arrange to continue their conversation that night through a window in the guarded quarters that the queen shares with Kay.

After obtaining the queen's permission, Lancelot tears the iron bars from the windows, enters her bedchamber, and consummates their love. Neither realizes that Lancelot cut his fingers on the bars, until the next morning when Guinevere awakens to bloodstained sheets and Meleagant's smirking accusations that the wounded Kay shared her bed. He demands that his father punish Kay and ensure that the queen is deeply humiliated, but Lancelot undertakes judicial combat after taking an oath on relics that the queen did not sleep with Kay. When Lancelot appears victorious, the king again asks Guinevere to separate them.

Lancelot again heads toward the Water Bridge to find Gawain and is lured away to captivity by a dwarf in Meleagant's employ. His party rescues Gawain from drowning at the Bridge and returns with him to Bademagu's court. Meleagant has a forged letter from Lancelot sent to induce them to return to Arthur's court, but when Gawain and the queen arrive there, they realize the deception.

The maidens in Logres have decided to hold a tournament and select husbands from among the victors, and when they learn that the queen has returned they ask Arthur for an unknown boon. The king, who has learned nothing, grants it unconditionally, but fortunately they wish only to have the queen at the tournament to draw a larger attendance. The queen obediently consents, and word of the tournament reaches Gorre, where Lancelot is being kept prisoner in the home of Meleagant's steward. Lancelot charms his hostess into allowing him to attend the tournament and lending him her husband's red arms. Taking an oath to return to prison, Lancelot attends the tournament and sweeps the field, until the queen, suspecting his identity by his performance, twice sends him a message to do his worst. Lancelot's performance becomes clownishly abysmal until he is the laughingstock of the tournament. Reassured of his identity and total devotion, the queen sends a message to him to do his best. His performance becomes so outstanding that the maidens will have no husbands but him, and the purpose of the tournament is defeated.

Lancelot keeps his word and returns to prison, and Meleagant builds a tower on a remote inlet, immures Lancelot therein, and leaves him to survive a year's imprisonment on starvation rations. Meleagant returns to Arthur's court and issues his challenge to fight Lancelot for the queen. Gawain offers to substitute for Lancelot if he cannot be found, and a year of searching by the court fails. Meleagant's young sister, the maiden who sought and obtained the head of the knight challenger, searches and finds Lancelot lamenting his fate in the tower. She rescues him and takes him away to her private house for several weeks, where she nurses him back to health.

Lancelot returns suddenly to Arthur's court as Gawain is arming for the duel for the queen. He rejects Gawain's offer to take his place and defeats, disembowels, and beheads Meleagant. As Lancelot is carried triumphantly away, the queen, who has kept her distance, is succumbing to her passion and planning to reward him by another tryst.

Interpretations

In all Chrétien's romances the material or subject matter is arranged and presented to convey meaning, and *Lancelot* can be interpreted in several ways.

At its simplest level *Lancelot* is an adventure story, a rich fusion of the tale of the abduction of Guennuvar in the *Life of St. Gildas* and of the adultery of Guinevere and Mordred in *The History of the Kings of Britain*. The action begins immediately and dramatically with the abduction of the queen, and the character of her unnamed rescuer is developed skillfully. In his adventures along the road to Gorre and afterward he is repeatedly humiliated or tempted and then reasserts himself as a man with a special mission. On the first day, after he mounts the cart and is jeered at by his hostess, he affirms his heroic nature by surviving the flaming lance and burning bed. On the second day he resists sexual temptation by his amorous hostess, who comments on his special qualities and quest. On the third day, after his humiliation at the games, the father and son recognize his mission when he lifts the tomb lid and establishes himself as the liberator of Gorre. On the fourth day after brief imprisonment between sliding doors, the rioting prisoners of Gorre acclaim him a hero. On the fifth day he beheads the knight who ridicules him for having ridden in the cart. In his sublime moment he crosses the sword bridge and defeats Meleagant, only to be humiliated by the queen and then by the crowd that takes him prisoner. He is reaffirmed by his night of love with Guinevere and his triumph over Meleagant in judicial combat, only to be abased again when Meleagant takes him prisoner. His devotion to the queen is proved by his humiliating performance at the tournament at her orders before he sweeps the field and departs, declining all maidens as his wife. His most abject humiliation after the cart is his imprisonment in the tower, before his great victory in the final battle, when he slays Meleagant and permanently liberates the queen. In this adventure story Chrétien uses great artistry in presenting violent battles, great perils, passionate interludes, a splendid tournament, all in context of the dominant theme of saving the queen, which runs from the beginning to the end.

In the modern sense of a romance, Chrétien carefully traces the progress of a love affair. At Camelot, the queen is aware that she has an admirer in Lancelot, whom she has never embraced, and her abduction reveals his devotion. At Gorre the couple undergo testing and estrangement, a sudden and more complete realization of their passion when each believes that the other has died and does not wish to go on living, remorse, reconciliation, and consummation of their love. At the tournament comes the ultimate testing and the queen's realization that they are totally one another's, so that when Lancelot returns to court she plans to see him again alone. Thus Lancelot leaves the court as her admirer and returns to court as the great love of her life.

In classical terms, *Lancelot* is also reminiscent of tales in Greek and Roman mythology of a woman captive in the Underworld. In her relationship with Bademagu and Meleagant of Gorre, Guinevere could be considered a Persephone abducted and imprisoned by a Pluto-like king in the realm from which none return. In her relationship with King Arthur, she could be considered an Alcestis sent by an uncaring husband like Admetus to take his place in the realm of the dead and restored to him by a Hercules in his employ. In her relationship with Lancelot she resembles a Euridice awaiting rescue from Hades by her lover Orpheus. Chrétien was familiar with these tales, and, like his treatment of love, they reflect the influence of Ovid in his works.[38]

In Christian terms throughout the romance there is a sustained struggle between the forces of good and evil, personified by a single hero and a single villain. There are Christian symbols in the tale of the knight who pursues the straight and narrow way, enduring humiliations and resisting temptations, and who views his tomb and elects his mission as a savior before entering the realm of the dead with bleeding hands, knees, and feet to liberate the prisoners therein. The analogy should not be carried too far: In Chrétien's romance Lancelot is a brave fighter and an ardent lover but too flawed by human passion to be a Christ figure; Meleagant is a vainglorious and sadistic young man, bent on evildoing, but not a devil; and the release of the captives in Gorre is a secondary theme, since their plight was tolerated for years until Guinevere joined their number, and Lancelot, in rescuing her, became incidentally their hero. But there are Messianic overtones to Lancelot's role as their rescuer and savior that are evocative of the Harrowing of Hell, as uncomfortable in religious terms as Lancelot's idolatry of the queen when he genuflects before her bed as if it were an altar, which show a Christian influence on the romance.[39]

Primarily, however, Lancelot is a study of love outside marriage. Three types of extramarital relationships are developed in Lancelot, and the characters are strongly influenced by all three, although they are mutually inconsistent.

The first relationship, purely physical, is that of the "old custom" of Logres and, to judge by Meleagant's outrage, of Gorre, whereby a knight who wins a lady in combat from her defender is entitled to possess her without consideration of her wishes or marital status. This rationale for rape is accepted by Kay, who is willing to stake his sovereign's wife in his wager that his prowess is superior to Meleagant's, by the lustful damsel who tempts Lancelot with a similar inducement to unchastity, and by Meleagant, who can only be deterred by his father's guards from violating the queen. It is not accepted by King Bademagu and is definitely rejected by Guinevere in her cold repudiation of Lancelot after he has most reason to expect her gratitude and affection for delivering her in combat from her abductor.

The second relationship is that of adultery, a violation of the marital relationship between husband and wife, in which the wife owes her husband total fidelity and obedience, whatever her personal feelings for him. Chrétien handles the idea that marriage is no impediment to courtly love by creating a triangle in which Arthur is seldom present and never informed of or ridiculed for his wife's involvement with her lover; the single interlude takes place far from his court and in an Otherworld setting. He also presents Lancelot as oblivious to any culpability in this relationship. Guinevere, however, is presented as a dutiful wife, well aware of its social and moral consequences,

[xxv]

particularly since for a queen adultery is also the crime of high trea-
son and punishable by death. Recovering from her confusion, she
heatedly denies adultery with Kay or promiscuous conduct and sends
for a champion to defend her reputation as a virtuous wife. Even in
such an Otherworldly setting, Meleagant does not hesitate to accuse
Guinevere of adultery in his desire to disgrace and degrade a woman
whom he is physically prevented from possessing, and King Bade-
magu feels entitled to require Guinevere to account for the suspicion
of such misconduct under his roof. Thus indirectly Chrétien conveys
his personal opinion that there are limits to how far a married woman
should go in rewarding a courtly lover and presents Guinevere, in
granting the ultimate favor, as having exceeded these bounds.[40]

The third relationship is that of courtly love between knight and
lady, again intensified because the lady is the queen, the paragon of
ladies, superior in all ladylike qualities as she is superior in rank, and
the more aloof and domineering by virtue of her position. This re-
lationship predominates and is most fully explored. Throughout the
romance Lancelot displays the qualities of the perfect courtly lover.
His courage and prowess are tested and proven in brutal trials, under-
gone because of his unswerving determination to find the most direct
way of rescuing her. His religious faith is shown by his piety at the
monastery. He shows courtesy and moderation in his dealings with
others he encounters during his travels and imprisonment. His word
is his bond, even when his vow to return to captivity leads to im-
prisonment in the tower. He is faithful to his lady throughout many
temptations, submissive to her caprices and unquestioning of her de-
cisions, patient when she turns against him, eloquent and charming
when permitted in her presence. His love for the queen inspires him
to feats of superhuman prowess and makes him prone to spells of rapt
contemplation of his loved one, fits of despondency, and adoration of
her person. Lancelot is extraordinarily tested to determine not only
whether he has the immense courage and prowess needed to rescue
the lady but also whether he is prepared to sacrifice his reputation for
such outstanding qualities at her demand. In the secret, other world
of this relationship the lady's love, given freely and without guilt, is
the sublime reward for the knight's sublime efforts to merit it.[41]

The rules and standards of these three relationships are as contradictory for the persons involved as is the immured Lancelot's appeal to the Holy Spirit to save him from the way the pagan goddess Fortuna is controlling his life, but throughout the romance the characters shift from one to another. Thus a queen abducted with her husband's consent for purposes of rape finds herself obliged to defend herself against charges of adultery brought by the would-be rapist, and to reward her lover physically and guiltlessly she would have to be, not in an Otherworld, but in another world.

Characterization

The most profound implications of the romance and its influence on literature arise both from the complexity of these relationships and from Chrétien's genius in creating human, believable characters that are consistent with, but transcend the stylized portraits of, the courtly lady and lover.

Chrétien's Lancelot is more fully and directly described than many of his other heroes. Bademagu calls him brave, noble, fair-minded, and gracious, and the narrator terms him as handsome as an angel when he recovers from his captivity. When not swept away by his violent hatred for Meleagant or his passion for the queen, he is calm, reasoned, serious, and unswerving in purpose. He is a devout Christian but at ease with the supernatural because of his fairy upbringing. Although traditionally in tales of courtly love the hero is inspired by love for the lady to feats of prowess that surpass those of ordinary men, Lancelot gives the impression of being nearly as outsized as Meleagant; he displays amazing strength and stamina throughout his trials. He can be as wily as Tristan; his insistence on taking an oath on Christian relics that the queen is not guilty of adultery with Kay when he knows that by Christian standards she is guilty of adultery is clever but not inspiring. He is brutally tough; the three horses he kills contrast strongly with Yvain's love of animals, and he threatens and terrifies a herald who recognizes him at the tournament. His adoration and veneration of the queen offset the image of the iron bars torn from stone with blood-stained fingers, but the image remains a powerful one; the number of women who desire him attest to his appeal, and it is in terms of his sexuality that he is tempted. Despite his buffoonishness at the tournament and two impetuous suicide attempts, Lancelot seems to be older and more mature than Erec, Yvain, and Perceval, who are young knights seeking to establish their reputations. Chrétien reveals at the end that Lancelot is older than Meleagant, with years more experience in sword play. He is a tough and seasoned warrior who has made his reputation; what is required of him is to sacrifice it. He never errs from naiveté or forgetfulness, only by assuming that others are as honorable as himself, but when the pattern of abduction, poisoned dressings, malicious accusations, forgery, and cruelty is finally established, he knows Meleagant's true worth and deals with him accordingly at the end.

In Meleagant Chrétien has created for Lancelot a consistent rival and nemesis; in *Lancelot,* unlike the other romances, the hero's actions and passions are focused on a single villain. Despite skirmishes with other knights, Lancelot has only one enemy, and one whose determination and treachery are pathological. In a brilliant twist on the creation of a villain, Chrétien has given Meleagant parallels with Lancelot so numerous that he might be Lancelot's dark mirror. Both are kings' sons and handsome, familiar with supernatural realms. Both are fighters jealous of their reputations; Meleagant is eager to establish his reputation by defeating Lancelot, and Lancelot wants to preserve his reputation by defeating Meleagant. Both are sexually obsessed with the queen: Meleagant is filled with lust and longing to humiliate and degrade her, and Lancelot is filled with desire and longing to adore and venerate her. Lancelot is tough with horses and heralds and his policy of never pardoning twice; Meleagant is sadistic, applying poisoned bandages to an injured man's wounds and starving Lancelot on foul food in the tower. Lancelot goes by the letter of the law in his judicial combat in the queen's defense, but Meleagant is all deceit in challenging Lancelot at court under the terms of their agreement when he himself has walled Lancelot in the tower. Both hate intensely and are determined to have the queen, and their struggle will be ended only by death.

Queen Guinevere is presented more flatteringly, but not more fully, in Chrétien's other romances. In *Erec* she presides over the marriage of Erec and Enide, and in *Cligés* she exhorts Alexandre to

allow her to arrange his marriage with Soredamors so that on that
honorable and firm foundation their love will long endure. In *Yvain*
she is portrayed as an affectionate wife, and in *Perceval* Gawain pays
special tribute to her noble qualities.[42] In *Lancelot* she is a beautiful
blonde, regally aloof, who behaves with exceptional discretion and
self-command. Perhaps to make her love affair more palatable, Chré-
tien portrays her as unappreciated; King Arthur, helplessly bound
by his word, allows her to be the pawn in Kay's power play, and,
although she can draw a huge crowd at the tournament, the court
seems indifferent to her fate. At the beginning of the romance the
queen knows that Lancelot cares for her, but the abduction brings
the affair into the open: by process of elimination courtiers who
were informed by Count Guinable of her murmur in Gawain's pres-
ence about an absent protector would have no difficulty determining
which of her two rescuers he would be (and much later the distraught
Lancelot shouts his love for the queen to his entourage). A certain
formality in Gawain's manner toward Lancelot as they set out to res-
cue the queen may imply that as the king's nephew he now realizes
the extent and implications of Lancelot's passion for the queen.[43] Led
defenseless to Gorre, the queen manages to enlist King Bademagu's
protection to preserve her virtue, and by charm and diplomacy sets
her own terms of captivity and becomes his favored dinner compan-
ion. She has a capricious streak and rejects Lancelot, for which she is
deeply contrite; her insistence that Lancelot humiliate himself twice at
the tournament, when once would have proved his identity and obe-
dience, and her mocking laughter at the infatuated maidens whom
she is depriving of a splendid husband, show an unattractive exulta-
tion in her power. Her poised comment upon receiving the news of
Lancelot's death publicly at the dinner table that she would indeed
have reason to grieve if any knight died in her service is belied by
her attempt to starve herself. She shows that she can match Lancelot
in ardor and intensity of emotion, but she blushes with mortifica-
tion upon discovery and condemns herself. Thus Chrétien greatly
transcends the conventional portrait of the remote and imperious
courtly lady that inspired the songs of the troubadours, creating a
lady of such beauty, intelligence, and discretion, who loves deeply
and despite her best efforts cannot conceal it, planning a tryst in her

husband's domain when she is constantly watched by courtiers who know that Lancelot loves her and whose support of her is at best luke-warm. Chrétien ends the tale with a resolution that is more tragic than joyous. Meleagant is dead, and Lancelot will be rewarded by a private visit with the queen, but Guinevere is not a courtly lady rewarding a devoted knight with her favors but a married woman and a queen capable of reciprocating her lover's passion in a situation where discovery seems inevitable.[44]

Continuations

Perhaps to forestall such a possibility, Chrétien may have intended *Lancelot* to end at that point, with the queen safely in Arthur's court and the night in Gorre a memory, an isolated interlude in an Other-world. The clerk Godefroy de Leigny, writing at Chrétien's direction, firmly states that the romance ends there and would be marred by continuations. But, like the *Story of the Grail,* Chrétien created a story and a cast of characters too fascinating and compelling to contain. Like Tristan and Iseut, Lancelot and Guinevere realized after Gorre that they were totally one another's; their love had intensified. Captivated audiences clamored for continuations. And, although courtly love evolved partly as a reaction to the Tristan legend and was superbly portrayed in Chrétien's romance of Lancelot and Guinevere, the seeds of tragedy he sowed therein proved far more destructive than in the Tristan legend. The tragedy developed in the continuations of *Lance-lot* that described the lovers' liaison when Lancelot was at Arthur's court. The triangle involving Tristan, Queen Iseut, and King Mark had an outcome that was confined to the principals: Tristan and Iseut died and King Mark was left to bury them with his realm of Corn-wall intact. In the continuations, the triangle involving King Arthur, Queen Guinevere, and Lancelot led to the destruction of the fellow-ship of the Round Table, civil war in Britain, and the downfall of Arthur and his kingdom.

Chrétien's romance of Lancelot was combined with the second of Chrétien's most popular themes: the quest of the grail, and incorporated into the prose Vulgate Lancelot-Grail Cycle, written ca. 1215–1235 and containing three narratives of Lancelot. In the first, the Prose *Lancelot,* themes of the *Knight of the Cart* are reworked and modified. Because of his desire for the queen, Lancelot begins to symbolize fallen human nature, so that his son Galahad emerges as the knight worthy to see the grail. The grail itself has been Christianized since Chrétien's time from a fish platter to a symbol of the sacraments. In this version Galahad is begotten by Lancelot when the Grail King Pelles deceives Lancelot into believing that his daughter Elaine is Queen Guinevere. (Chrétien's description of Lancelot's stay with Meleagant's young sister may be a precedent for this episode of Lancelot's involvement with a young maiden.) The second narrative, the *Queste del Saint Graal,* portrays Lancelot as repentant of his sin and thus able to find the Grail Castle, but the vision of the Grail is granted only to Galahad and Perceval and Bohort. In the third narrative, the *Mort Artu,* Lancelot resumes his affair with the Queen, with the disastrous consequences of civil war and alienation from Arthur.[45] In the English fourteenth-century romance *Le Morte Arthur,* Lancelot and Guinevere are ambushed in her bedroom by Gawain's brother Agravain. While Lancelot rescues Guinevere from burning at the stake, his killing of Gawain's brothers Gaheries and Gaheriet makes Gawain his implacable enemy. Gawain and Arthur besiege Lancelot until they are forced to return to England to save Guinevere from Mordred, who has attempted to marry the queen. Gawain is killed in the last battle, Mordred is slain, Arthur is wounded and ferried to Avalon, Guinevere becomes a nun, and Lancelot spends the last seven years of his life as a hermit at Glastonbury.[46] Malory incorporated this material into his fifteenth-century English *Le Morte Darthur.*[47] Malory's many successors include Tennyson, and his nineteenth-century poems *The Idylls of the King;* T. H. White, who wrote the twentieth-century novel *The Once and Future King;* and Lerner and Lowe, the composers of the musical *Camelot.* Chrétien created a tale of a love affair that each generation seems compelled to retell in the light of its own times. It is fascinating to see how many aspects of the subsequent romances of Lancelot and Guinevere are foreshadowed in the subtleties of Chrétien's seminal work.

Translator's Note

The Manuscript Tradition

Chrétien's *Lancelot* has been preserved in seven manuscripts and, of Chrétien's works, may have the most uncertain manuscript tradition. Three manuscripts are complete: C, or B.N. 794; T, or B.N. 12560; and V, or Vatican 1725. Manuscript C is available in an edition by Mario Roques; manuscript T is the basis for the Foerster edition. Four are fragments: F, or B.N. 1450; A, or Chantilly 472; E, or the Escorial manuscript; and Garrett 125 (at Princeton University).[48] This translation is based mainly on the Roques edition of manuscript C, which is satisfactory and readily available, but it incorporates certain significant variants from other manuscripts and many of the 250 corrected lines by Albert Foulet.[49] Manuscript C contains important omissions, such as the reference to Camelot in v. 33a and the two steps Lancelot hesitates before mounting the cart in v. 360b, and some inconsistencies: in it the queen's murmured aside as she leaves court (v. 209) is addressed to the king. In an uncertain manuscript tradition there will always be disputes about the best resolution of variants, but the goal is a readable coherent text.

Translating Old French

No translation is a substitute for reading the original, but translations are needed by people who have not achieved sufficient mastery of a foreign language to read the original with ease and appreciation but who wish to become acquainted with an important work. Old French is as difficult for a modern French reader as Old English is for a modern English reader, and a native English speaker may require years of study to be able to read and appreciate modern French literature. No two languages correspond precisely, and translations are not a suitable tool for advanced studies of grammar or nuances in vocabulary of the source language, for which the original should be used.[50] Sometimes a precise equivalent does not exist, and so the translator must settle for the best match possible.

Chrétien de Troyes wrote in Old French, a language encompassing several dialects used between the ninth and late fifteenth centuries that has significant differences from modern French or English for purposes of translation.[51] First, Old French retained from Latin a simplified two-case declension system; different forms were used to indicate whether certain nouns were subjects or complements of the verb. Thus the word order of the sentence was more flexible than the usual subject-verb-complement structure of a modern French or English sentence, because the ending or form of the noun was supposed to indicate whether it was a subject or complement.[52] As an additional complication, because of scribal error and an ongoing breakdown of the declension system it was not uncommon for subject and verb to disagree in number or for confusion to exist concerning subject and complement. While Chrétien's vocabulary was extensive for his time, Old French had not experienced the period of tremendous enrichment in vocabulary in the sixteenth century through DuBellay, Ronsard, and the other poets of the Pléiade, and of subsequent organization by Malherbe. By comparison with the literature of the last four centuries, Chrétien conveys complex and rich meaning with a vocabulary that is relatively limited.[53] These considerations are important in conveying the substance of the original text.

Considerations of Form

Form, however, is a very important part of any literary work and is altered or ignored at peril. The idea or substance originates in the mind of the author, but the form shapes its expression at its earliest stages and is an intrinsic part of the creative process. A poet who chooses a highly structured form of verse accepts the constraints imposed by the metrical and rhyme scheme and phrases his thoughts accordingly. Chrétien's verse not only shapes his expressions but establishes the pace of his romances—a forward movement sustained by rhyme and meter and arrested at key points by rephrasing and repetition, a poetical device that seems redundant in prose.[54] His language in his day was considered modern, even innovative, and his works are enlivened by puns, parodies, and proverbial expressions; word play that loses its essence if it is not translated idiomatically. Moreover, while Chrétien was undoubtedly capable of writing prose, his work sprang from a tradition of verse, rhymed poetry, and song meant to be presented orally to an audience. The great prose romances were not written until fifty years after his time in the thirteenth century. Thus a prose translation can convey Chrétien's story but cannot give an impression of his style or artistry.[55]

Chrétien himself wrote narrative poetry in *octosyllabe*, rhymed unaccented couplets with eight syllables per verse. While he used a considerable amount of assonance and consonance, he showed an increasing preference for rich or perfect rhymes of one, two, or more syllables, including homonyms (Godefroy de Leigny used a higher proportion of perfect rhymes and a much higher proportion of homonyms).[56] Sometimes, particularly with lists, the rhyme seems to dictate the choice of vocabulary.[57] Chrétien was an innovator in making *octosyllabe* more flexible; he used enjambment or run-on lines and broke the couplet by making two lines that rhyme part of two different sentences. The closest English equivalent to *octosyllabe* is iambic tetrameter, a framework of about sixteen syllables with two rhyming words. Within this framework, the translation must convey the essentials of the original couplet from Old French, a Latin language, to English, a Germanic language.[58] This form of verse fits *octosyllabe* well; there is no room to make additions but no pressure to make omissions. Occasionally, minor liberties must be taken with vocabulary in the search for equivalents, but the translation is accurate and closely follows the Old French text.

Among the benefits of verse translation, the pace of the romance is restored, proverbial expressions retain their pungency, and poetical devices and word play can often be conveyed. An additional benefit is that in the classroom and elsewhere rhyme and meter have proved remarkably effective in fixing the tale in mind and capturing the attention, so that many readers grasp the plots of Chrétien's works more quickly in verse translation, understand and empathize with the motivations of his characters, and are prepared and eager to pursue more comprehensive analyses of his works. Thus the additional effort of rendering the form as well as the substance has been well rewarded.

LANCELOT

or

THE KNIGHT OF THE CART

PROLOGUE

MY lady of Champagne* wills
that I begin to use my skills
for a romance; at her proposal,
as one at her entire disposal
in all that he can do on earth,
I gladly start it with a dearth — scarcity or lack of something
of eulogy to interpose.
Though one to praise her, if he chose,
might mention, as I will attest,
she is the lady who can best   10
all living ladies in the way
the breeze of April or of May
surpasses humid fogs and mists,*
I'm not one of those eulogists
who praise their lady's excellence.
Shall I proclaim with eloquence
that, as one diamond, bright and hard,
is worth amounts of pearl and sard,
so is the countess worth of queens?*
No, I would utter no such paeans;   20
in spite of me, they are correct.
But her commands have more effect
herein than all my pains and art.
The story of *The Knight of the Cart:*
now Chrétien begins his book.
Material and theme he took
the way the countess made them known,
while adding little of his own
except his effort and intention.   29

An asterisk (★) indicates that a corresponding textual note can be found in the notes to the text.

[1]

30 THEY say that once at the Ascension*
30a toward Caerleon King Arthur wended;*
his court was sumptuous and splendid.
The writer shall begin the plot
33a when he held court at Camelot,*
33 as splendid as a king deserved.
34 The king, with dinner done and served,
did not withdraw from his companions.
The hall was filled with many barons;
together with them was the queen,
and I believe there could be seen
fair, courteous ladies thereamong,
40 conversant in the Gallic tongue.*
Kay,* who directed their repast,
was dining with his servers last.
While Kay was seated at his fare,
a knight* arrived at this affair,
who came to court well armed and dressed,
with all the weapons he possessed.
The armored knight, on entering,
proceeded till he reached the king,
who was among his barons, seated,
50 and told him, leaving him ungreeted,
"King Arthur, in my prison cells
are ladies, knights, and demoiselles
of your own household and your land.
I do not bring the news first-hand
because I mean to give them back.
I've come to tell you that you lack
the resources and power and might
to come and save them from their plight,
and never, till your dying day,
60 can you assist them any way."
The king replied he must endure it,*

if he could find no way to cure it,
although the news was deeply grieving.
The knight pretended he was leaving;
he stayed before the king no more
but turned and headed for the door,
though he did not descend the stair.
Instead he stopped and said from there,
"King, if your court has ever known
a single knight, just one alone,   70
in whom you've confidence so sweeping
you'd trust the queen in his safe-keeping,
so she would follow, with so good
a body-guard, into this wood,
I should await him without fail.
All captives in my land and jail
I promise that I shall surrender,
if he is able to defend her
and to return her undeterred."
Within the palace many heard;   80
the court was filled with consternation.
Kay overheard this invitation
among the servers while he dined;
he left his meal straightway to find
King Arthur, whereon he commenced
as if he were indeed incensed.
"King, I have served you royally,
devotedly, and loyally;
I'll take my leave, and go away,
and serve no longer from this day.   90
I've no desire or disposition
to serve you now in this position."
To hear this left the king desponding;
but, when more equal to responding,
the king immediately pressed:
"Are you in earnest or in jest?"
In answer, "Good lord king," Kay spoke,
"there is no need for me to joke.

[3]

This is indeed my resignation.
100   I ask no other compensation,
no other wage of any kind,
but now I have made up my mind
to leave your service in a hurry."
"But is it from contempt or fury
that you would leave us, seneschal?"
the king asked, "Stay as usual;
remain at court, for I profess
there is no thing that I possess
in this world that I would refrain
110   from giving to you to remain."
"No need," Kay said, "I would decline
a bushel of pure gold and fine,
were it to be my daily share."
The king was wholly in despair,
and so he went to see the queen.
He said, "My lady, have you seen
what boon the steward would receive?
For he has asked to take his leave;
my court's no longer of his choosing.
120   I don't know why he is refusing.
What he will not, at my behest,
he'll promptly do at your request.
Dear lady, since he will not deign
to stay for me, have him remain
for your sake; find him and entreat,
and even grovel at his feet.
I shall not have one happy day
if I part company with Kay."
King Arthur sent the queen along.
130   She found the steward with the throng,
and when she reached the seneschal,
she said to him before them all,
"Kay, I am terribly distressed
and shocked to learn of your request.
What I've been told is shattering:

[4]

that you desire to leave the king.
What has come over you and why?
Your sense and manners seem awry,
and that is not their usual way.
I ask you to remain here, Kay;   140
I do implore you to abide."
"Forgive me, lady," he replied,
"however I would not remain."
The queen entreated him again,
and all the knights as one concurred.
Kay said her efforts were absurd,
and she was wasting energy.
The queen, despite her high degree,
went on to fall down at his feet.
In turn Kay started to entreat   150
the queen to rise, and she forbore;
never would she rise from the floor
until he did as she insisted.
Kay swore he would, and he desisted,
although the king must first agree
to grant his wish immediately,
which she herself must also grant.*
She answered, "Kay, whatever you want
both he and I will soon bestow,
now come, and we shall let him know   160
on that condition you will stay."
The queen, accompanied by Kay,
came to appear before the king.
"Sire, I have kept Kay tarrying,
although I met much opposition,
but he is yours on one condition:
whatever he asks, you will comply."
King Arthur heaved a joyful sigh
and said he was Kay's to command,
no matter what he might demand.   170
Kay said, "Now I shall tell you, sire,
what is the favor I desire

and you have pledged will be accorded,
for I shall think me well rewarded
when I receive it by your grace:
because you have agreed to place,
the queen in my care, as you swore.
We shall pursue that warrior
who waits for us within the wood."
180   King Arthur sadly said he could,
because he never broke his word;
in grief and anger he concurred,
as his face openly expressed.
The queen was terribly distressed.
Throughout the household people sighed
that foolishness, conceit, and pride
had motivated Kay's demand.
Taking the queen's hand in his hand,
the king began to say to her,
190   "My lady, now without demur
with Kay you must go dutifully."
Kay said, "Entrust the queen to me
without a shadow of a doubt,
for I shall lead the queen back out
quite safe and sound in every way."
King Arthur handed her to Kay,
who led her off; the others hurried
after the two, all deeply worried.
Soon they had armed the seneschal;
200   his horse was led out of its stall
into the courtyard, alongside
a palfrey for a queen to ride.
The queen went where the palfrey waited;
it was not restive, agitated,
or pulling hard upon its rein.
So, crushed and heaving sighs of pain
the sad queen mounted, saying low
so none would overhear and know,
"Oh, dear,* if you but knew of it,

[6]

I think you never would permit   210
Kay's leading me one step from here."
She thought her murmur was unclear,
but Count Guinable near her horse
could hear her protest and remorse.
When she rode off, there was such grieving
by those who saw that she was leaving,
she might have been dead on her bier.
They thought she would not reappear
among them all her lifetime long.
The steward, terribly headstrong,   220
led her to where the knight attended.
Yet nobody felt so offended
to get involved by following,
till Sir Gawain spoke with the king
his uncle, privately but riled.
"Sire, you have acted like a child
to my complete astonishment.
If you heed my admonishment,
since they are scarcely on their route,
the two of us can give pursuit   230
with those who wish to join our train.
I personally cannot refrain
from following them on the spot.
It would be wrong if we were not
to follow them each way they turn,
at least until the time we learn
about the queen's experience
and how Kay fares in her defense."
"Let's go, dear nephew," said the king,
"you've said a very courteous thing,   240
and since this plan is one you sought,
command the horses to be brought,
bridled and saddled, to your side,
so we need only mount and ride."
And soon the horses were brought near
with saddles, harnesses, and gear.

[7]

The king was first to mount his horse,
then Sir Gawain, and in due course
the others mounted, hurry-skurry.
250   All wished to come, but in the flurry
each rider went the way he chose,
both men in armor, there were those,
and many others were unarmed.
The lord Gawain was riding armed;
he had two squires, and on their right
each led a charger of the knight.
As they approached the forest's verge,
the party saw Kay's horse emerge.
They recognized it as it went
260   and noted both its reins were rent,
torn from the bridle on its head.
In solitude the charger sped.
Its stirrup leather was blood-spattered,
its saddle cantle wholly shattered.
The people saw it was converted
to fragments and were disconcerted
enough to wink and nudge and poke.
But far ahead of all these folk
the lord Gawain was riding fast.
270   When very little time had passed,
a knight* appeared at walking gait
upon a horse in such worn state
that it was panting, spent, and tired,
and lathery as it perspired.
He hailed Gawain first, on their meeting,
then Sir Gawain returned his greeting.
The knight, who knew the lord Gawain,
came to a halt to ascertain,
"My lord, can you not see as yet
280   my horse is weary, drenched with sweat,
and of no further use to me?
I think that these two steeds I see
belong to you, and so I pray,

[8]

with solemn promise to repay
this boon and service of your own,
that you will either give or loan
a steed to me, as you elect."
The lord Gawain replied, "Select
your preference and take either steed."
The knight, who was in desperate need,   290
did not select the better charger,
the finer, handsomer, or larger.
He mounted and began to ride
the charger closest to his side;
immediately he forged ahead.
His cast-off charger fell down dead.
He'd ridden it at such a length,
he overstrained and taxed its strength.
The knight, without a bit of rest,
tore through the wood, and spurred, and pressed.   300
Behind him Sir Gawain made haste
in hot pursuit of him and chased
until he'd ridden down a mound.
He rode a long way on, and found
the charger dead: the one, outright,
that he had given to the knight,
and hoofprints in great quantity,
and shattered shield and lance debris
profusely scattered overall.
It looked like a tremendous brawl   310
with many knights participating.*
He found it highly aggravating
that he had not been there as well.
He did not linger a long spell
but galloped on without a break
until he chanced to overtake
the knight alone on foot, who paced
completely armed with helmet laced,
shield hung from neck, sword buckled smart,
and he had come upon a cart.   320

[9]

THE CART

CARTS were used then in just the way★
   that pillories are used today,
because each good town that would store
three thousand carts today or more
in those days would have had one cart,
and this one was the lot and part,
as pillories are in our time,
of all who lead a life of crime:
of murderers and traitors fell,
330   those who in legal combat fell, ★
and thieves who prey on those they meet
and take their assets by deceit
or force: swindlers and highwaymen.
A criminal was carted then
through all the streets, and, when he crossed,
his property and rights were lost.
At court no one would hear him hence
or welcome him with deference.
In those days that is what carts meant.
340   They were so cruel a punishment,
it was first said, "Whenever you meet
a cart or see one on the street,
do cross yourself with upraised arm
and pray God keep you safe from harm."
The knight on foot, without a lance,
pursued the cart in its advance,
and on the shafts the knight beheld
a dwarf★ who, like a driver, held
a long horse switch clasped in his hand.
350   The knight went to him to demand,
"Dwarf," he said, "if my lady queen
passed by this place and you have seen,
then for the love of Heaven, tell."
The low-born dwarf, despicable,

not wanting to give an account,
replied to him: "If you will mount
upon the cart that I am guiding,
by morning you may learn some tiding
about her and about her fate."
He went his way and did not wait   360
or slow the cart in any way.   360a★
With only two steps of delay   360b
to his mischance, the knight complied,
for, sadly, he was mortified
and did not leap right in, but waited,
and he will deem himself ill-fated.
Because, as Love and Reason part,★
the last says not to mount the cart,
and as she voices her dissent,
she warns and chides him to prevent
his doing anything of shame
to merit deep disgrace and blame.   370
Thus, not within his heart is Reason,
but in his mouth, to dare so reason;
Love is enclosed within his heart
and orders him to mount the cart.
As Love has willed it, in he leapt.
Disgrace he'll heedlessly accept,
since Love so orders and prefers.
The lord Gawain came, using spurs,
and riding to pursue the cart.
The seated knight gave him a start.   380
He was amazed by what befell
and said: "Dwarf, if you're able, tell
whatever you know about the queen."
The dwarf said: "If you will demean
yourself as badly as this knight,
come sit with him, if you think right,
and I shall carry you with him."
When Sir Gawain heard plans so grim
he thought them utterly absurd

[11]

390 and would not mount, for he averred
he would be anything but smart
to trade a charger for a cart.
"But go wherever pleases you,
for where you go I shall go too."

THE FLAMING LANCE

AT that they went along the road,
two in the cart and one who rode.
Their way together was the same.
As night began to fall, they came
upon a castle, and know well
400 it was a splendid citadel.
All three men entered through one gate.
The people's wonderment was great
about the carted knight he brought.
They did not whisper what they thought,
for, young and old and great and small,
they booed him loudly, one and all,
throughout the streets and shouted jeers.
The knight heard many slights and sneers
and insults cried with virulence.
410 All questioned, "To what punishments
is this knight going to be conveyed?
Will he be hanged, will he be flayed,
or drowned, or placed on thorns and burned?
Tell, dwarf his driver, what you learned,
in what crime did he come to grief?
Is this man a convicted thief,
a murderer, a man defeated
in legal combat?" they entreated.
The dwarf drove him in silence, dodging
420 their every question, to his lodging;
Gawain was riding in pursuit,

[12]

on toward a tower upon their route,
which faced the town and was at hand.
Upon one side was meadowland;
upon the other rose the keep,
above a cliff, gray-brown and steep,
and falling sharply to the vale.
On horseback, on the tumbrel's trail,
Gawain rode through the tower wall.
They met a maiden in the hall,   430
and she was beautifully attired.
No one around was so admired
for beauty, and they saw a pair
of younger maidens, very fair
and well bred, coming in her train.
As soon as they saw Sir Gawain
they greeted him with great delight
and then inquired about the knight.
"Dwarf, what crime did this knight commit
that you drive him like one unfit?"   440
The dwarf, unwilling to impart
the reason, made him leave the cart
and left when he was on the ground.
They did not know where he was bound.
The lord Gawain dismounted too.
Then squires came and disarmed the two.
The maiden had two cloaks of vair
brought in the hall for them to wear.
When it was time for them to dine,
the meal was well prepared and fine.   450
The maiden came and took a seat
next to the lord Gawain to eat
beside that knight throughout the meal.
The two knights had no cause to feel
they ought to seek a better place.
The maiden honored them with grace;
her company was a delight
throughout the evening into night.

When they had eaten all they cared,
460   the maiden had two beds prepared
within the hall, both long and high.
Another bed was placed thereby,
richer and fairer than the rest
because, the story does attest,
its comforts were unlimited:
all one could fancy in a bed.
When it was time that they withdrew,
the maiden took her guests, the two
whom she would lodge in that abode;
470   two wide and lengthy beds she showed,
and both the beds were very fair.
"Two beds are made up for you there,
but only he who earns the right
may use the nearest bed tonight;
it was not made up for your slumber."
The knight who rode the cart of lumber
responded he was simply scorning
the maid's injunction and her warning
and meant to treat them with disdain.
480   He said: "I want you to explain
why it is a forbidden bed."
Without a pause the maiden said,
for she expected him to ask,
and promptly took the knight to task:
"Your questioning is out of place.
A knight is covered with disgrace
on earth once he was in the cart,
so it is not his rightful part
to ask the question that you pose
490   or, specially, to seek repose,
for soon he might be ill-repaid.
I did not have it richly made
for you to lie abed tonight.
You would be bitterly contrite
if such a thought should cross your mind."

[14]

"Soon you will see how I'm inclined."
"I'll see?" "Indeed you will." "Then do it."
"Although I don't know who may rue it,"
the knight responded, "by my head,
I mean to lie upon the bed,   500
no matter whom it may displease,
and to recline there at my ease."
Once he had lain his armor by,
he sought the bed, both long and high
by half an ell than either bed.
It had a yellow samite spread,
a starred and golden-hued brocade.
The cover's lining was not made
of skinned vair but of sable fur;
a spread a king might well prefer   510
became his cover as he lay.
The bed was not of thatch, or hay,
or straw, or rushes, or old mats.
At midnight, from the ceiling slats,★
a lance dropped like a thunderbolt,
the iron first, as if to bolt
the knight's flanks through the yellow spread,
the sheets of white, and then the bed,
while he reclined on its expanse.
There was a pennon on the lance   520
which was aflame; the fire it set
spread to the sheets and coverlet,
until at last the whole bed blazed.
The iron of the lance tip grazed
the knight's side as he lay therein,
so it removed a little skin,
but he was virtually undamaged.
The knight sat up in bed, and managed
to quench the blazing flames and fume,
and hurled the lance out in the room;   530
throughout it keeping to his bed.
Once more the knight laid down his head

[15]

and fell into as sound a doze
as when he first was at repose.
Next morning, at the daybreak hour,
the maiden who was of the tower
had Mass arrangements undertaken
and had the knights arise and waken.
When Mass was chanted in each part,
540   the knight once seated in the cart
proceeded melancholically
to a window looking on a lea
and gazed out over field and land.
The maid had come as well to stand
beside the other window pane
and had conferred with Sir Gawain
in privacy for a short spell.
I don't know what they had to tell
or what their words were, or their meaning,
550   but while the three were standing, leaning
out of the window, they beheld
a litter past the field, propelled
along the river, and inside
a knight was carried; alongside
the litter three maids raised lament.
Behind it a large party went;
there was an outsized knight preceding.
Upon his left this knight was leading
a lady who was beautiful.
560   The knight beside the window sill
perceived this lady was the queen.
He fixed his eyes upon the scene
intensely and with great delight
as long as she remained in sight.
When he could not see her at all,
he felt an urge to take a fall
and lie crushed at the tower's base.
He'd fallen halfway through the space
when Sir Gawain saw him go slack

and told him, as he pulled him back: 570
"Please calm down, sir, and Heavens above!
never again start thinking of
an act with idiocy so rife!
You are so wrong to hate your life."
"He is so right," the maid replied.
"Is he not known both far and wide
for the misfortune fate imparted
upon the day that he was carted?
So he must long not to survive:
he is worth more dead than alive.   580
From now on he will live abased,
despised, and wretched, and disgraced."
Immediately the knights called for
their arms and armed themselves for war.
The maiden showed her courtesy,
concern, and generosity,
for after she had finished jeering,
and scoffing at the knight, and sneering,
she gave him both a horse and lance
for love and from benevolence.   590
The two knights took their leave of her;
well-mannered as both riders were,
they hailed the maiden and departed.
The route whereon the two knights started
was where they'd seen the party last;
no one addressed them as they passed
out of the town to intervene
with haste where they had seen the queen.
They crossed the fields fast for her sake,
but found they could not overtake*   600
the party, which rode on apace.
They went into a closed-in place
and came upon a well-paved road,
so through the forest bounds they rode
until about the hour of prime.
Beside a crossroad, at that time,

[17]

they found a maiden,* whom they greeted,
and each knight asked her and entreated,
if she knew, and were not mistaken,
610   to where the queen was being taken.
The maiden answered knowledgeably:
"Now, if your promises to me
are generous enough in scale,
then I can put you on the trail,
show you the straight way to the site,
and name for you the land and knight
who leads her, but he must withstand
great pain who seeks to reach that land!
To suffering he must submit
620   before the day he enters it."
The lord Gawain said to the maid:
"I promise, Heaven grant me aid,
that I shall do all in my power
to serve you at your chosen hour,
I promise without reservation;
tell me the truth without evasion."
The knight who had been in the cart
made her no pledge in counterpart
of everything within his power;
630   unfalteringly, he did vow her,
as one whom Love makes rich, and bold,
and powerful in ways untold,
that he would honor and fulfill
her wishes and be at her will.
"So I shall tell you both," she stated,
and this was what the maid related:
"Lords, Meleagant of Gorre, a knight,
the king's son, huge and filled with might,
has just contrived to overwhelm
640   the queen and took her to his realm,*
from where no stranger may return,
but in the country must sojourn
in exile and in servitude."

"Where is this land?" the knight pursued.
"Wherever can we find the way?"
The maiden answered: "I shall say,
but manifold impediments
and obstacles await you hence,
and passes filled with misadventure.
It is no easy place to enter,   650
unless the king allows you through;
his name is King Bademagu.
Yet you can enter nowadays
through two extremely dangerous ways.
There are two treacherous and fell
passages to his citadel.
The Water Bridge we call the first,
because the bridge has been immersed.
Above the bridge the water-flow
is just as deep as that below,   660
no more, no less; the bridge's beam
is at mid-level in the stream,
one and one-half feet side to side
and just as thick as it is wide.
A passage you might well refuse,
yet it's less dangerous to choose.
I shall not tell you its adverse
respects; the other bridge is worse.
It is so dangerous a span*
it's not been crossed by any man,   670
for it is like a cutting sword.
So everyone is in accord
and calls this passage the Sword Bridge.
By now I have fulfilled my pledge
and told you all the truth I can."
The knight inquired about each span:
"Please, maiden, tell us how to find
both ways, if you will be so kind."
The maiden answered, as he sought her:
"This path's straight to the Bridge in Water,   680

[19]

and over there that path runs toward
the other way, the Bridge of the Sword."
The knight who once rode in the cart
had this proposal to impart:
"I shall allow you to decide.
Select one path on which to ride,
and I shall take the other, sir.
Please take the way that you prefer."
"My word," replied the lord Gawain,

690   "both passages to that domain
are dangerous and hard to use,
and so I cannot rightly choose.
I do not know which one to take,
yet waivering is a mistake
when you allow me to select.
The Water Bridge I shall elect."
"So I shall take the path remaining:
the Sword Bridge path, without complaining,"
the other said, "and I agree."

700   When he had said these words, the three
commended themselves, noble-hearted,
to God's protection and departed.
She saw they would be leaving soon,
and said: "You each owe me a boon
which you must grant me as I name it
whenever I decide to claim it.
Take care that you do not forget."
"Sweet friend, we won't forget our debt,"
both knights were very prompt to say,

710   and each one went his separate way.
The cart knight brooded at some length,*
a man without defense or strength
against Love and her tyranny.
His thoughts were of such quality,
no feeling of himself persisted,
he did not know if he existed,
could not remember his own name,

[20]

where he was bound, from where he came,
or whether he was armed or not.
Except for one thing, he forgot   720
all others totally, and all
but her were lost beyond recall.
He thought so much of her alone,
things went unseen, unheard, unknown.

THE GUARDIAN OF THE FORD

BUT in the meantime his swift horse
bore him upon no crooked course,
rather the most direct and sure,
and chanced to bring him to a moor.
Upon this moor there was a ford;
on the far bank, with lance and sword   730
a knight in armor guarded it.
This knight positioned opposite
had a young maiden at his side.
She had a palfrey there to ride.
The knight in reverie who brooded
had not tired of it or concluded.
The afternoon had run its course.
The knight's extremely thirsty horse
saw the clear water and ran toward
the sparkling and limpid ford.   740
The guard called from the other side:
"Sir knight, I guard the ford," he cried,
"I am forbidding it to you."
The other neither heard nor knew,
because he was still lost in thought.
The horse sped on, because he sought
to reach the water, bright and clear.
The guard called out to make him hear,
"If you are wise, you'll turn away;

[21]

750 this ford is not your passageway!"
and swore by heart within his chest
to strike him down if he progressed.
The knight was deafened by his trance.
The horse swerved from the field's expanse,
leapt in the ford, and slipped his bit,
and started drinking out of it.
The guard said he would pay him back,
nor would the hauberk on his back
or shield protect him from a wallop.

760 He urged his horse into a gallop
and from a gallop to a run,
and struck the knight so he was spun
flat into mid-ford by the toss;
the ford he would not let him cross.
The shield hung round his neck by cord
and lance fell with him in the ford.
But when the knight could feel the stream
he started like one in a dream
who wakes bewildered when he's slept.

770 In the cold water, up he leapt.
He heard, and saw, and wished to know
whoever could have struck the blow.
He saw the guard and yelled: "Reply,
vassal who struck me, tell me why,
when I did not see you near me
and did not do you injury?"
The guard said: "Faith, you did indeed,
for did you not refuse to heed
the triple warning that I roared

780 that you were not to cross the ford,
especially when I called it out
as loudly as my voice can shout?
You must have heard my challenge thrice,"
he told the knight, "or at least twice,
yet you went in the stream I barred.
I said that I would strike you hard

[22]

if once I saw you in the wet."
The knight said, whom he had beset:
"Damned if I ever saw or heard!
It may have possibly occurred,   790
while I was lost in reverie, — *lost in thought*
that you denied the ford to me,
but I shall cause you greatest pain
if I get one hand on your rein."
The guard replied: "What do I care?
Come seize my rein now, if you dare,
and hold me by it. In our clashes
I think a gauntlet full of ashes
of all your menaces and pride."
"I ask no more," the knight replied,   800
"because, whatever may ensue,
I'd like to get my hands on you."
He went in mid-ford to restrain
the guard, his left hand on the rein,
thigh in his right hand firmly seized,
and then he pulled, and tugged, and squeezed
the guardian's thigh so very hard
that he protested, for the guard
felt shortly that he would be lame,
his thigh wrenched wholly from his frame.   810
He pleaded to be left at ease
and said to him: "Knight, if you please,
fight with me as an equal match.
Take up your shield and lance, and catch
your horse, and come and joust with me."
"I shall not do so, certainly!
I think you will give me the slip
the moment you escape my grip."
The guard was truly mortified
and said: "Knight, mount your horse and ride,   820
for I can promise faithfully
that I shall not escape or flee.
I take it very much amiss

[23]

that you would slander me like this."
The knight repeated what he'd heard:
"First you will have to pledge your word,
for I insist you take a vow
you will not flee or dodge me now,
but you will be above reproach
830   and will not touch me or approach,
until you see I have remounted,
and I believe I shall be counted
kind to release you from my clutch."
The guardian vowed it, inasmuch
as by then he could do no more.
The knight first heard the oath he swore,
and then retrieved his shield and lance,
which floated in the ford's expanse
a long way downstream on their course,
840   and then returned to get his horse.
Remounting after his mishaps,
he took his shield up by the straps,
and then he put the lance at rest.
To their encounter both knights pressed
as fast as horse could bear them hence.
The knight who was the ford's defense
attacked the other first; the guard
struck at the knight extremely hard,
so that his lance was wholly shattered.
850   The knight struck him so that he battered
the guardian flat into the ford.
Over his frame its waters poured.
The knight, when he resumed his place,
dismounted, feeling he could chase
one hundred foes as difficult.
He drew his steel sword at his belt;
the guard leapt up and drew his blade,
which was agleam and finely made,
and man to man they fought unquelled.
860   Their shining golden shields were held

before themselves and used as cover.
They took no pauses to recover;
they worked well with their swords and chose
to give each other heavy blows,
and fought so long, the knight of the cart
could feel disgrace within his heart.
It boded ill, the knight reflected
about the way he had selected,
if he required so long a fight
to overcome a single knight.   870
If he had found the day before
one hundred knights his match for war
within a valley, he contended
that they could never have defended
themselves against him. Sad and cross
because his blows were such a loss,
and he was weak, his day a waste,
he rushed the guardian in great haste,
till he gave way and took to flight,
surrendering the ford outright,   880
however much against his will.
The knight pursued the guard until
the guardian fell upon his palms.
The carted knight swore without qualms
the guard, as he saw, was untoward
to make him fall into the ford
and snatch him from his reverie.
The maiden in his company
could hear these threats against her knight
and asked him in tremendous fright   890
please not to kill him, for her sake.
He said he would, make no mistake,
and could not show the knight compassion
when he'd been shamed in such a fashion.
And so the knight, with drawn-out sword,
came on the guardian of the ford.
In terror he began to moan:

[25]

"For God's sake, sir, and for my own,
be merciful as I request."

900 "God love me," the knight acquiesced,
"No man has done such harm to me
and in God's name sought clemency
that, for God, what were his affronts,
I would not show him mercy once.
I shall have mercy, which is right,
for I should not refuse outright
the pity you would have conferred,
but first you must give me your word
to go to be a prisoner

910 whatever place I may prefer
when I have summoned you to go."
He promised, in the depths of woe.
"Knight, out of generosity,
since he has asked for clemency,"
the maid said, "and you did concur.
If you've released a prisoner
at any time, free him for me.
Release him to me prison-free.
In turn, and at the proper hour,

920 I'll grant whatever in my power
you care to ask me to bestow."
So by her words she let him know
her actual identity.
He freed him in her custody.
She felt great shame and agonized
for fear she had been recognized;
she did not want to have him know.
The knight immediately turned to go.
Commending him to God, the pair

930 requested leave to go from there.

THE AMOROUS HOSTESS

HE gave permission, then he set
off until evening, when he met
a maiden, beautiful, and charming,
well-dressed, and polished, and disarming,
proceeding on her way to meet him.
The lovely maid began to greet him,*
correct in manners and polite.
"God keep you, maid," replied the knight,
"both sound of body and of mind."
She said: "Nearby, sir, you will find   940
my house prepared for you, well kept,
if you are willing to accept.
I offer it conditionally,
for you must go to bed with me,
and so I offer and present it."
Though many would have thanked, and meant it,
the maid five hundred times, much gladdened
by such a gift, the knight grew saddened,
and he responded in this way:
"I thank you for a place to stay   950
and do appreciate such ease.
About the shared bed: if you please
I could do very well without it."
The maiden answered: "Do not doubt it,
I shall not lodge you otherwise,
I give you warning, by my eyes."
The knight could do no better than
to grant it and accept her plan,
although it grieved him to the heart.
If he feels wounded at the start,   960
his bedtime grief will be intense
and wound the maid who leads him hence.
Perhaps the maid will love him so
she will refuse to let him go.

[27]

He vowed to do her will in all;
she led him to a bailey wall,
since he was willing to agree.
As far away as Thessaly
no finer bailey could be found;
970   high walls, deep water all around
enclosed the place, by men vacated,
except the man whom she awaited.
She'd had fine rooms built in its wall
and an immense and spacious hall
and thus constructed her abode.
Along a riverbank they rode
and came to where they were to stay.
So they would have a passageway,
the bridge was lowered to the ground.
980   They crossed the drawbridge span and found
the hall, wide open and tile-covered.
The door was open, they discovered.
On entering, the knight and maid
found a set table overlaid
by a large tablecloth's expanse.
The food was brought there in advance,
and lighted candles had been braced
in candelabra and were placed
with silver goblets, gilded fine,
990   and two pots, one of mulberry wine
and one of white wine, strong and heady.
Two basins of hot water were ready
on one end of a bench nearby them,
so they could wash their hands and dry them,
for in the hall they found elsewhere
a towel, embroidered, white and fair.
And yet they neither saw nor found
a man-at-arms or squire around,
and so no servants were revealed.
1000   Alone the knight removed his shield
from his neck, hung it on a hook,

[28]

and after that was done he took
his lance and placed it on a rack.
He sprang down from his horse's back.
The maid dismounted and alighted.
The knight approved and was delighted
she had not waited with persistence
for him to come to her assistance.
As soon as she had reached the ground,
she ran into a room and found   1010
a cloak of scarlet fabric, short,
to wrap the knight she would escort.
Although by then the stars shone bright,
the hall was not as dark as night,
because to dissipate the gloom
large, twisted candles filled the room
and shed great brightness as they burned.
After the maiden had returned
and put the cloak she was to lend
around his neck, she said: "My friend,   1020
the water and the towel are here,
although no servants will appear
to offer them, for you will see
nobody in this room but me.
So you may wash your hands and sit
wherever you consider fit.
The hour and meal are both completed,
so wash your hands and then be seated."
"Most willingly," the knight complied.
The maiden sat down at his side.   1030
The food and drink were shared and passed
until they rose from their repast.
When they had risen from the board,
the maid said to the knight: "My lord,
go and amuse yourself outside,
if you don't mind, but only bide
as long as you think I require
to seek my bed and to retire.

[29]

You would do well to make the best
1040   of it and not to be distressed.
Then you may enter undeterred,
if you intend to keep your word."
The knight replied to her concern:
"I'll keep my promise and return
when I believe the time is right."
For a long interval the knight
walked in the courtyard and delayed
until he had to seek the maid,
because his word held him in thrall.
1050   The knight went back into the hall
but did not find the one who made
herself his sweetheart, for the maid
had disappeared and was not there.
He could not find her anywhere.
"Wherever she may be enclosed,
I'll search until she is disclosed,"
he said, and he delayed no more
by reason of the oath he swore.
He went into a room while seeking
1060   his friend and heard a maiden shrieking:
the very maid he visited,
with whom he was to go to bed.
He saw the door had been unlatched
to the next room, and as he watched
a knight assailant, rough and lewd,
held the maid down, completely nude,
across the bed. The screaming maid,
quite certain he would bring her aid,
cried loudly: "Help! Help! Knight, my guest,
1070   I have no one but you to wrest
this man from me. If you aren't swift
1072   to come and rescue me, and lift
1072a   this man off me, and make him rise,
1072b   this knight, before your very eyes,
will shame me uninhibited.

[30]

You are supposed to share my bed
as you have promised solemnly.
Is he to have his way with me
before your eyes, by force and might?
Please make an effort, noble knight,
and help as quickly as you can."
The knight could see the evil man   1080
had bared the maiden navel-high
and was distressed to see him lie
upon her naked body nude,
which filled him with disquietude,
profound embarrassment, and ire
but not with envy or desire.
Now, there were porters at the entry:
two knights in armor, standing sentry,
with naked swords, and backed by four
stout men-at-arms to bar the door;   1090
each held an axe so overblown
that it could hew a cow's backbone
as easily as if it were
a twig of broom or juniper.
The knight stood still before the door.
"Oh, God, what can I do?" he swore,
"the reason that has brought me here
is no less than Queen Guinevere.*
On that great mission, for my part,
I must not have a rabbit's heart,   1100
when I am on a quest like this.
Should I accede to Cowardice
by borrowing a heart that weak,
I shall not reach the goal I seek.
I'll be disgraced if I remain.
Now I am filled with great disdain
that I spoke of remaining here.
My heart is very dark and drear,
and I could die of shame and wrong
that I have lingered here so long.   1110

[31]

May Heaven's mercy be denied
if I have said it out of pride,
better to die with honored name
than to live out a life of shame.
Now, if the doorway had no guard,
would I be held in high regard
if they allowed me, with compliance,
to pass beyond without defiance?
Without a lie, the worst man living
1120   would enter in without misgiving.
Meanwhile this poor maid keeps repeating
her pleas for mercy, and entreating
and calling to me long and loud
about the promise I had vowed,
and covering me with vile reproach."
So the knight started to approach ★
the doorway, thrust through head and neck,
and then looked upward as a check.
He saw the sword blades as they flew,
1130   and so he hastily withdrew.
The knights had moved at such high speed,
they could not halt their blows at need.
Upon the ground the sword blades crashed;
the pieces flew as they were smashed.
Once that the swords were valueless,
the knight esteemed the axes less
and held them in far less respect.
He leapt on one man, then the next,
and struck the nearest men–at–arms
1140   with both his elbows and his arms,
and flattened them, and laid them low.
Meanwhile the third man missed his blow.
The fourth attacked with such a stroke,
the axe came slicing through his cloak,
through his chemise and flesh of white,
into the shoulder of the knight,
so that the blood began to drip.

[32]

Quite undeterred by such a clip,
the hurt knight in no way impugned
or raised complaint about his wound,   1150
but came on, lengthening his stride,
and seized the head on either side
of the knight who was using force
against his hostess. In due course
he wished to leave, his oath fulfilled.
He seized his temples, and he pulled
the man up, willingly or not.
The man who missed him reached the spot
with utmost speed, and raised his axe
to split the knight's skull wide in cracks   1160
to run from cranium to teeth.
The skilled knight blocked it from beneath
with the assailant of the maid;
he was disjointed by the blade
between his neckbones and his shoulder.
Well schooled in self-defense and bolder,
the knight reached for the axe and grasped it,
abandoning the man who clasped it
once he had torn it from his fist,
because he needed to resist   1170
the knights beginning their attacks
and three men each armed with an axe,
and they were cruel and resolute.
He leapt, to ward off their pursuit,
between the bedstead and the wall,
and said: "Come at me, one and all!
If you were seven men and twenty
you would have battle and aplenty
while I remain in this redoubt,
for you will never wear me out!"   1180
The maiden watched this exercise.
"You need fear nothing, by my eyes,
henceforth wherever I may be,"
and she dismissed immediately

[33]

the knights and axemen, all of whom
departed promptly from the room;
no one objected or entreated.
When they were gone, the maid repeated:
"Sir, you have saved me well and true
1190   from my entire retinue.
Come, I shall lead you therewithal."
So hand in hand they sought the hall.
The knight found it no pleasanter
and wished he could be rid of her.
In center hall a bed was made.
The sheets were not unclean or grayed
but white and ample, of fine stuff.
The mattress padding was not rough,
filled with cut straw or of such ilk.
1200   A coverlet of flowered silk
made of two cloths was overspread.
The maiden lay down on the bed
without removing her chemise.
The knight took greatest pains to ease
his shoes and clothes off and retire.
His anguish caused him to perspire,
but as his anguishing repels him,
his promise conquers and impels him.
Now, is this force? Well, tantamount.
1210   His promise calls him to account
and warns him of the vow he made:
perforce he must lie with the maid.
The knight retired by degrees*
without removing his chemise
because she had not done as much.
He made sure that they did not touch.
He turned his back to her and shrunk*
away as silent as a monk
to whom speech is prohibited
1220   when he is lying on his bed.
He did not look to either side

[34]

or straight ahead. Dissatisfied,
he could not feign to be elated.
Why? Since his heart was dedicated
to another, it had not reacted.
Not everybody is attracted
to someone nobly born and fair.
He cannot lend his heart elsewhere
because he has one heart alone
he can no longer call his own.   1230
Devoted to another face,
his heart remained all in one place,
for Love, who rules all hearts, so deems.
All? Only those that Love esteems.
Those whom Love deigns to rule on earth
should think themselves of greater worth.
His heart has left Love so impressed,
Love rules it over all the rest,
and Love has filled it with such pride
that I have no desire to chide   1240
if he rejects the one Love banned
while he obeys Love's least command.
The maid knew and could clearly see
he did not want her company
and gladly would relinquish it.
She had no other requisite
and said, since he was not inclined
to touch her: "If you do not mind,
sir, I shall leave you and instead
seek out my room and go to bed.   1250
Then you will be much more at ease,
for I believe that I displease
by both my charms and company.
Don't think me lacking courtesy
for telling you my thoughts outright.
I hope you find repose tonight,
for you have kept your word so truly,
I would ask more of you unduly.

[35]

You have no further obligation.
1260   To God I give you commendation,
and I shall go." She rose to leave,
which did not cause the knight to grieve;
he gladly let the maid depart.
The one he loved with his whole heart
was someone other than the maid,
to whom it clearly was conveyed.
Into her room she went, subdued,
and went to bed completely nude,
and told herself: "Since I began
1270   to know knights, there is not one man,
save him that I would think as fine
as one-third shilling Angevine,*
for I believe and I presume
the quest he wishes to assume
is such a great one that no knight
has dared to undertake a fight
in which such perils may impend.
God grant he sees it to the end."
At that she fell asleep and lay
1280   until the dawning of bright day.

THE GILDED COMB

THE moment that the morning broke
she rose as soon as she awoke.
The knight awakened from his rest,
armed and equipped himself, and dressed
without delaying to be served.
The maiden entered and observed
he was equipped for war or fray.
"I hope the dawn brings you good day,"
the maiden greeted him on sight.
1290   "You also, maiden," said the knight.

[36]

He said how eagerly he sought
for her to have his charger brought.
The maiden had them fetch the steed
and said: "I wish I could proceed
with you along this thoroughfare
some distance, sir, if you would dare
escort me, keeping to the ways
and customs that in early days
were kept before we could be found
within the realm of Logres' bound,   1300
wherein we were incorporated."
The customs that had been instated
in olden days were of a kind
that if a knight should chance to find
a maid or wench someplace remote
he would prefer to cut his throat
than cause the girl humiliation,
if he would keep his reputation,
and if he forced her in that place
he was in permanent disgrace   1310
forevermore in every court.
But were another to escort
the maiden, and he chose to fight
and won her from the other knight,
then he could have his way unblamed
and would not be abased or shamed.
This custom is why she declared
that if the knight agreed and dared
to be her escort, riding armed,
so that she would remain unharmed,   1320
then she would go where he preferred.
The knight replied: "I give my word
that you will never be coerced
unless that person harms me first."
She said: "I want to go with you,"
and had her palfrey saddled too.
Her orders promptly were obeyed.

The palfrey was brought for the maid
and the knight's horse led in the court.
1330   They mounted without squires' support
and started riding at high speed.
She talked to him, who paid no heed,
for while his pleasant thoughts relieved him,
her conversation only grieved him,
so he ignored each opening.
Although Love kept reopening
the wound she dealt, which was agape,
he bound it with no plaster tape,
because good health had no allure.
1340   He had no interest in a cure
and sought no plaster or physician*
until it was in worse condition,
but he would seek her willingly. . . .
The couple rode unswervingly
along the straightest trails revealed
into the middle of a field
which had a fountain bubbling.*
There was a stone nearby the spring.
Someone—who to me is unknown—
1350   forgot and left upon the stone
a comb of gilded ivory.
Not since the time of Ysoré*
has sage or fool seen one so fair.
The ivory comb contained some hair.
The lady who had combed her head
left half a handful she had shed.
The maiden noticed on her own
the fountain and the nearby stone
and hoped they would be unobserved;
1360   onto another path she swerved.
While savoring his train of thought
and the great pleasure that it brought
at first he was not so astute
to see she'd led him from his route,

[38]

but finally, when he perceived,
he feared that he had been deceived;
her detour was a ruse employed
to take the long way and avoid
some place that might be peril-laden.
He said to her: "Come back here, maiden.   1370
You chose your pathway incorrectly.
No one, I think, rode on directly
once he had ridden off this road."
"We would do better if we rode
this way," she said, "I know it well."
The knight replied: "Mademoiselle,
I cannot guess what you suppose;
you can see clearly that I chose
the straightest way and beaten trail,
and since I did, I shall not fail   1380
to follow it or turn aside.
Please come along, for I shall ride
the trail to which I have adhered."
So they went on until they neared
the comb that lay upon the stone.
He said: "I never have been shown
as fair a comb as I now see."
The maiden said: "Give it to me."
He answered her: "As you see fit,"
bent down at once, and lifted it.   1390
Once that he held it in his hands,
he gazed a long time at the strands,
and thought about the comb, and mused.
The maiden laughed aloud, amused.
He saw and asked the maid to tell
what she had found so laughable.
"Hush, I shan't say what's on my mind."
"Why not?" "I am not so inclined."
He heard and made her an appeal
as one who truly did not feel   1400
a woman who has loved a man

[39]

or man who loves a woman can
betray his word in any part.
"If you have loved with your whole heart,
then by your lover I implore,
do not conceal it anymore;
I beg of you and I insist."
"You're so sincere I can't resist,"
the maiden said, "I shall reply,
1410   and in no manner shall I lie.
If I have knowledge or discretion,
this comb was in the queen's possession,
and also, I believe the hair,
so bright and shining and so fair,
caught on the comb's teeth and between
came from the head of that same queen.
They sprouted in no other field."
Responding to what she revealed,
"But there are many a king and queen,"
1420   he said, "which queen is it you mean?"
She said: "Upon my word and life,
I'm speaking of King Arthur's wife."
When the knight heard, he lacked the force
to keep from bending over his horse.
He had to keep his body low
and lean upon his saddlebow.
The maiden saw him weak and dazed
and was astonished and amazed,
because she feared he might collapse.
1430   If she was frightened by his lapse,
don't blame the maid or raise complaint.
She thought he was about to faint,
and he was nearly in a swoon
and might have fainted very soon.
He felt such pain within his heart
that he had lost the greater part
of his fresh color and his speech.
Dismounting, she made haste to reach

[40]

his side as quickly as she might
to steady and assist the knight.   1440
For anything that could be found,
she would not have him fall to ground.
He saw her and was filled with shame.
"Tell me the reason why you came
to stand before me and dismounted?"
Don't think the maid would have recounted
the actual reason why she went;
he would have felt embarrassment
and been extremely hurt and pained
to hear the truth, so she refrained   1450
from saying why she came in fact.
She said to him with utmost tact:*
"I came to get this comb we found,
so I descended to the ground;
so very greatly I desired it,
I could not wait till I acquired it."
He wanted her to have the gift
and gave it, managing to lift
the hairs out with a gentle hand
and did not break a single strand.   1460
No eye will fall in contemplation*
on objects of such veneration,
because he worshipped and embraced them.
A hundred thousand times he placed them
against his eyes, mouth, face, and brow,
and no joys did he disavow.
They made him rich and well at ease.
They went between skin and chemise
within his chest close to his heart.
He would not trade them for a cart   1470
of carbuncles or emerald beryls.
Electuaries mixed with pearls
he did not need, or theriac,
or fear an ulcerous attack,
pleurisy, ills by other names,

[41]

or need Saint Martin or Saint James!
He placed so much faith in the hairs
that he required no aid of theirs.
Now, what was in them to admire?
1480 I will be thought a fool and liar
if I speak truth about the hair.
When at Lendit there is full fair,*
goods overflowing every stall,
he would not want to have it all,
and this is proven truth and sound,
if this hair had been left unfound.
And gold—to truth I am confined—
a hundred thousand times refined
and melted down, would to the sight
1490 appear as dark as blackest night
beside the finest summer day
of all this summer's bright array
to anyone who could have spied
the gold and hair placed side by side.
Why should I give a long account?
The maid got swiftly on her mount
and took the comb. The knight, elated,
was joyful and inebriated
about the hair tucked in his chest.
1500 Beyond the moor the couple pressed
into a forest, and they tramped
a side road till the path grew cramped.*
In single file they had to ride
because two horses side by side
could never ride that cut abreast.
The maiden rode before her guest
along the straight path unrestricted.
Where the side road was most constricted
the pair saw an approaching knight.
1510 She recognized the man on sight
the moment that he came in view.
"Sir knight, see that man coming through

the forest, armed and battle-ready?
That warrior has planned already
to carry me off unopposed.
I know full well what he supposed
should such a circumstance arise.
He loves me and is far from wise,
for personally this knight has sought me
and through the messages he brought me;   1520
he has long sued for my affection
and yet has only met rejection.
God help me, I shall be deceased
before I love him in the least.
Nothing can make me love this knight.
I know how great is his delight;
so joyful has this rider grown,
I might already be his own.
Now I shall see if you can save me.
Now we shall see if you act bravely.   1530
Now we shall see and now detect
if as an escort you protect.
If you can come to my defense,
then I shall say without pretense
that you are brave and valiant."
He said: "Come, come," and these words meant
as if he said: "What I have learned
has left me wholly unconcerned.
You have no need to be afraid."

THE GAMES

WHILE they rode on, the knight and maid   1540
kept on conversing in this tone.
The knight approaching them alone
did not come riding slowly there.
He galloped up to meet the pair

and was delighted to make haste.
He thought his efforts were no waste;
presumed good fortune made him boast
on seeing her whom he loved most.
When they were not too far apart,
1550   he greeted her with lips and heart.
"Now may the one for whom I languish,
who gives me least joy and most anguish,
be welcome from wherever she's faring."
She should not be with words so sparing
as to refuse upon their meeting
to pay lip service to his greeting,
for silence would not have been right.
It was important to the knight
to have her greet him with restraint,
1560   although her lips received no taint
nor did it tire the demoiselle.
If he had jousted very well
that moment at a tournament
he'd not have been so self-content
or felt he'd won as much acclaim,
or honor, or renown and fame.
Because he was extremely vain
he seized her by the bridle rein
and said: "I'm leading you away.
1570   I have sailed well and true today*
and have arrived at a safe harbor.
My problems I no longer harbor;
I've come from peril into port,
from great distress to great disport,
from wretched pain to splendid health;
my wishes are fulfilled in wealth,
to find you in a situation
where I can keep my reputation
and carry you away at last."
1580   The maiden answered: "Not so fast;
I am escorted by this knight."

[44]

"Then you are in a sorry plight,
for I shall lead you off at once,"
the knight continued his affronts.
"This knight will eat a keg of salt
before he chooses to find fault.
There's no man I could not subdue,
from whom I could not conquer you.
Now I have found you with such ease,
however much it may displease,   1590
I'll lead you off before his eyes;
whatever defense he can devise."
The words he spoke did not incense
the other by their insolence.
Without a boast or taunting word
his own firm challenge he preferred:
"Sir, do not act in so much haste
and let your words be such a waste;
speak only after you've reflected.
Indeed, your rights will be respected,   1600
once you acquire some over her.
The maiden is a traveller
escorted by me, as you've known,
whom you detain; leave her alone.
As yet she need not be concerned."
The knight took oath he would be burned
were she not his against her will.
The other said: "I would do ill
to let you lead the maid away,
so you will join me in a fray.   1610
Our combat would be doomed to fail
if we attempt it on this trail.
We cannot fight here, to be sure.
Let's find a highway, field, or moor."
The knight replied he asked no better.
"Your offer suits me to the letter,
and you are not the least mistaken.
This narrow pathway we have taken

[45]

is not for combat of this kind.
1620 My charger would be too confined;
before I end this turn I make,
I fear one of his legs will break."
The turn was difficult indeed
but did no damage to his steed,
which stood unscathed upon the path.
The knight exclaimed: "I feel such wrath
that we did not come face to face
within an open, public place,
with witnesses that could attest
1630 which one of us can fight the best.
Now come and search, for near at hand
we'll come upon a tract of land
that's open, broad, and unconcealed."
So they proceeded to a field.
In it were maidens, knights, and dames,
and they were playing different games
because it was a lovely spot.
The games the people played were not
all pastimes of lightheartedness.
1640 Some played backgammon, others chess,
and others different games of dice.
Although these pastimes did suffice
for many people, others flung
themselves in games they'd played when young.
In carols, rounds, and reels they danced,
they somersaulted, and they pranced,
they leaped and sang whole songs and snatches,
and some engaged in wrestling matches.
Across the meadow to one side
1650 there was an aged knight astride
a sorrel steed that was from Spain.
His saddle, harness-straps, and rein
were golden, and his locks were gray.
With hand on hip in such a way
that he looked boldly at his ease,

[46]

he watched the games in his chemise
because the weather was so fair.
He wore a mantle lined with vair
of scarlet cloth across his back.
Beside a path there was a pack   1660
of twenty-three armed men in force,
each on a sturdy Irish horse.
The moment that they saw the three,
the people stopped their revelry,
and shouts arose from every part:
"Look at the knight towed in the cart!
Stop every dance and every game
as long as he is here in shame.
Cursed be the one who seeks to play
or to amuse himself this day,   1670
and cursed be anyone who deigns
to play as long as he remains!"
While everybody called and jeered,
the gray-haired knight's young son appeared,
who loved the maiden and had shown
he now considered her his own.
"Sir, I am in a joyful spirit;
whoever wants to hear may hear it,
for through God's help I have acquired
what I have always most desired.   1680
He'd not have done as great a thing
if He had had me crowned a king,
nor would I feel such gratitude
or win as much as I've accrued.
How fine and lovely is this present!"
"I'm not sure it is yours at present,"
the gray-haired knight informed his son
concerning what he thought he'd won.
The son replied immediately:
"Lord, don't you know, sir? Don't you see?   1690
Don't doubt that she is mine to claim,
for in that wood from where I came

I met her just now. As I see,
the Lord was leading her to me,
and so I took the one I wanted."
"I am not sure she has been granted.
Behind her I can see a knight;
I think he'll challenge you to fight."
While these assertions were expended,
1700   the dances and the carols ended.
The games and revels were arrested,
because they hated and detested
the knight they saw while at their play.
The knight rode up without delay
behind the maid, and as he came
he spoke thus: "Knight, you have no claim
to her, so let the maiden be.
Dare press your claim, and instantly
I'll fight for her and overthrow it!"
1710   The old knight said: "Now, didn't I know it?
Dear son, stop holding her restrained
and let her ride on undetained."
These words displeased her would-be lover,
who vowed he would not hand her over.
"If I succumb to such a ploy,
may Heaven never grant me joy.
The maid is mine, to my belief,
and I shall keep her in my fief.
I'll break my shield straps, my enarmes,★
1720   and leave off trusting in my arms,
or in my body, sword, or lance,
before there is a circumstance
in which I let my sweetheart go."
The older knight responded: "No,
you may not take part in a fray,
no matter what you choose to say,
for you are overly reliant
upon your prowess. Be compliant
and let her go, as I directed."

[48]

The young knight haughtily objected: 1730
"Am I a child to fill with fright?
I boast the sea surrounds no knight,
and there are many in its flow,
so good that I shall let her go
or whom I think such a contender
I could not soon make him surrender."
His father told him: "I agree,
and I believe you readily,
dear son, you trust so in your might.
You may not test it on this knight;   1740
I shall not have it, not today."
The young knight answered him this way:
"I would act shamefully indeed
to pay your counsel any heed,
and cursed be he who would believe it,
and seek the battlefield, then leave it,
not having valiantly competed.
I know you wish to see me cheated.
Dealing with kith and kin has dangers,★
for better terms are had from strangers.   1750
My valor would be better shown
in some land other than my own,
where no one knew me and could find
a way to make me change my mind,
for you have harried me and pestered,
and your rebuke has deeply festered.
He who reproaches any plan
devised by woman or by man
and warns them they will surely rue it
makes them more eager to pursue it.   1760
If in the slightest you deter me,
no further joy may God confer me,
for I shall fight though you are hostile."
"Now by Saint Peter the Apostle,"
the father said, "I cannot fail
to see prayers are of no avail,

[49]

and by the faith I owe that saint
I'd waste my time to raise complaint,
but I shall soon devise a way
1770 that will compel you to obey,
because you will be overridden."
The knights approached as they were bidden
to carry out their lord's decrees.
The old knight ordered them to seize
his own son, whom he could not guide,
and told them: "I shall have him tied
before this fight will come to pass.
You are my liegemen here en masse
and owe me love and loyalty;
1780 by everything you hold from me,
so I entreat you, and I rule.
My son is acting like a fool
and is exceedingly ambitious
to feel he can oppose my wishes."
The knights said they would hold him tight,
and he would be less keen to fight
once that they had him firmly held,
and he would also be compelled
to yield the maid, though it displeased him.
1790 So, by the arms and neck, they seized him
and held him up for ridicule.
"Now don't you think yourself a fool?"
his father asked him, "Face the facts:
your strength and power for attacks
or jousting cannot be employed,
whether or not you are annoyed,
and what be your regret of it.
So you will do as I think fit,
if you are wise and will be guided.
1800 Do you know what I have decided?
If it will mitigate your sorrow,
throughout this day and then tomorrow
we two shall ride in this knight's train

and follow him through wood and plain,
each at an amble on his horse.
There may be something in due course
in his demeanor that I find
induces me to change my mind
and let you put him to the test
and fight with him as you request."   1810
The old knight's son had to agree.
The knight could see no remedy
and said he would allow them there,
but they must follow as a pair.
When this adventure was revealed
to all the people in the field,
remarks arose from every part.
"Did you see? By the knight of the cart
today such honor has been won,
he leads the love of our lord's son;   1820
our lord is following behind.
To tell the truth, our lord must find
some merit that this knight displayed
to let him lead away the maid.
There'll be a hundred imprecations
on those who leave their recreations
on his account. Back to our fun!"
They played their games and danced and spun.

THE TOMBS

THE knight immediately wheeled
and stayed no longer in the field.   1830
The maiden did not feel inclined
to stay there and be left behind,
so they rode fast and with persistence.
The son and father, from a distance,
pursued them; they rode through a mown

meadow till the hour of none
and found, within a pleasant place,
a church and, off the chancel space,
a cemetery that was bounded
1840 by walls and totally surrounded.
The knight, who was no fool or clod,
went in on foot to pray to God.*
The maiden held his horse's rein
until he had come back again,
and after he had said his prayer
he went back in the open air.
A monk of ancient years and guise
appeared before his very eyes.
When he had met the monk, the knight
1850 inquired in tones low and polite
about the walls, what lay inside.
A cemetery, he replied.*
"May Heaven grant you true reward.
Escort me there." "With pleasure, lord."
He took him in the monastery
and led him in the cemetery
among the most imposing tombs
that could be found as far as Dombes
or as Pamplona, each engraved
1860 to show for whom the tombs were saved
with writing to identify
the names of those therein to lie.
The knight himself, upon his own,
read out the names as they were shown,
discovering "here will lie Gawain,
here Lionel, and here Yvain,"
and after these three, many a name
of chosen knights of great acclaim,
the most esteemed knights, and the best
1870 this land and other lands possessed.
One tomb seemed new, of marble stone;
its splendid workmanship outshown

the tombs around it, one and all.
The knight then gave the monk a call:
"What purpose are the tombs here serving?"
The monk responded by observing:
"The tombs' inscriptions you have seen;
if you know what the letters mean
then you know what they specify
and what these tombs must signify." 1880
"The largest, who is designated?"
The hermit never hesitated:
"I'll tell for whom it is intended.
It's a sarcophagus more splendid
than any that was ever done,
and neither I nor anyone
has seen a richer tomb or rarer.
It's fair outside and inside fairer,
although that is irrelevant
and wholly insignificant. 1890
You'll not see the interior,
for seven strong, superior,
huge men must use their strength and skill
to open up this tomb at will.
It's covered by a slab of stone,
and it takes seven men full grown
with greater strength than we are gifted
for this stone cover to be lifted.
These words are written on the stone:
'He who can raise this stone alone 1900
with his own body's strength shall then
release the women and the men
who are imprisoned in the land
where foreign serfs and lords are banned *
from leaving once they penetrate.
Nobody has returned to date.
In that land strangers are detained;
as prisoners they have remained,
whereas the natives come and go

[53]

1910   at their discretion to and fro.' "
At once the knight went up to seize
the slab and lifted it with ease,
more smoothly than ten would acquit
themselves with all their strength in it.
The monk was filled with so much awe
he nearly fell down when he saw
this marvellous accomplishment.
He'd not see its equivalent,
he thought, throughout his whole life long.

1920   He told him: "Now I greatly long
to learn your name, sir. May I know?"
To which the knight responded: "No,
not by the faith I have professed."
The monk said: "I am much distressed.
If you would tell your name to me
you'd do me a great courtesy
and might have very much to gain.
Who are you and from what domain?"
"I am a knight, and I was born

1930   within the realm of Logres' bourn.
I think that will be adequate.
And, if you please, reiterate
who will lie in that sepulcher?"
"It will be the deliverer
of all caught in the trap that gapes
in that realm from which none escapes."
When the monk told it all and ended,
to God above he was commended
and to His saints all by the knight,

1940   who went as quickly as he might
back to the maiden in his care.
The aged brother, white of hair,
accompanied them from the church ground
back to the path, which they soon found,
and while the maiden was remounting,
the monk was occupied recounting

the knight's achievements, one and all,
within the cemetery wall,
and he beseeched the demoiselle,
if she had learned his name, to tell.   1950
She said she did not know his name;
one thing alone she dared to claim:
that no knight living was his peer
wherever the four winds blow and veer.
The maiden hurried off to find
the knight and left the monk behind.
The knights who followed them around
arrived before the church and found
the monk alone. "Sir, tell us please,"
asked the old knight clad in chemise,   1960
"if you have seen a knight who led
a maiden going on ahead?"
"It is no trouble to recount
a fully accurate account,
for they just left this monastery.
The knight was in the cemetery.
So wondrous were the things he did:
a great tomb has a marble lid
and effortlessly, all alone,
he lifted up that slab of stone,   1970
so its interior was seen.
The knight has come to save the queen;
for certain he will rescue her
and every other prisoner.
You know it too," the brother said,
"because you frequently have read
the slab whereon the words appear.
There never was a knight his peer.
None could be found of mortal birth
or in a saddle of such worth."   1980
And then the father asked his son:
"What do you think of what he's done?
In courage is he not elite

[55]

to have accomplished such a feat?
You see where the rebukes belong
and whether you were right or wrong.
For Amiens and all within
I would not let you fight with him,
although, before you were deterred,
1990   a battle with yourself occurred.
Since we will be far from astute
if we continue our pursuit,
let us return from where we went."
The son responded: "I consent;
pursuit can be of no avail.
Let us go back along the trail
whenever you are pleased to ride."
The maiden, clinging to his side,
because she wished the knight would mention
2000   his name and pay her some attention,
time and again pressed and appealed
to have his name known and revealed,
till he was filled with irritation.
"Did I not tell my land and nation:
King Arthur's realm?" replied the knight.
"By all I owe God and His might,
and by the faith that I proclaim,
I shall not let you know my name." ★
She asked permission to depart;
2010   he granted it with his whole heart.

THE STONY PASSAGEWAY

THE maiden left for her abode.
Without companionship he rode
until it was the close of day.
As he was following the way
with vespers past, as compline verged,

[56]

out of a wood a knight emerged
where he had hunted deer and chased.
He rode up with his helmet laced,
his venison was strapped and corded—
such meat as Heaven had afforded—   2020
upon a horse of iron gray.
The vavasor asked him to stay;
he hurried up to meet the knight
and said: "Sir, it will soon be night,
and so you should have no objection
to seeking shelter and protection;
the reasons for it are compelling.
Not far from here I have a dwelling,
and I shall promptly take you there.
No one will give you better care   2030
or any better place to rest,
and I shall gladly do my best."
"I shall be glad as well," he said.
The vavasor sent on ahead
his son to make their dwelling look
its best and hurry up the cook
to greet their guest in fitting state.
The young man did not hesitate
but instantly obeyed and went,
most faithfully and most content,   2040
at highest speed to their abode.
The two men followed down the road
but at a far more leisured pace,
until they reached the lodging place.
The vavasor had in the house
a gracious lady as his spouse,
five sons in whom they both delighted:
three were but youths and two were knighted,
two daughters, lovely and well bred,
who were still maidens and unwed.   2050
That land was not where they were born,*
but they were prisoners in its bourn

and long held in captivity.
The place of their nativity
was Logres' realm. The vavasor
led the knight to his courtyard door.
The lady ran outside to meet him;
daughters and sons leapt up to greet him.
They vied to serve his every need
2060 and helped the knight down from his steed.
The brothers five and sisters fair
gave their own father little care.
They knew that he would think it best
for them to serve their honored guest.
They welcomed him with great respect.
He was disarmed and then bedecked
with the same mantle that was worn
by his host's daughter, who had torn
the cloak from her own neck and pressed
2070 the wrap upon the knight her guest.
At supper he was nicely served,
about which I remain reserved,
but at the end of the repast
they felt they could begin at last
to talk of many a concern.
The vavasor first wished to learn
who his guest was, from where he came,
but he did not inquire his name
when asking him who he might be.
2080 "I am from Logres," instantly
the knight informed the vavasor.
"I've not been in this land before."
Such words as these could but appall
the host, his wife, and children all.
They were astounded and distressed
and started saying to their guest:
"It's so unfortunate you came.
Good sir, it is a dreadful shame,
for you will be in our position.

From this day forward, your condition   2090
will be exile and servitude."
"From where are you?" the knight pursued.
"Sir, we are from your native land.
So many Logrian lords are banned
from going home and live enslaved.
Cursed be a custom so depraved,
and its upholders be accursed,
that outsiders should be coerced,
once they have entered, to remain
imprisoned here by the domain.   2100
Whoever seeks to enter may
but afterward is forced to stay.
There is no question, I believe,
that you can ever hope to leave."
He said: "I shall leave, if I can."
The host replied: "What is your plan?
You think that you can take to flight?"
"I mean to do all in my might,
and if it pleases God, I shall."
"Then fearlessly the others all   2110
will leave, if one man who fights fair
evades this prison and this snare.
All others who are in subjection
can leave this land without objection
whenever they are so inclined."
The vavasor then brought to mind
that it was being said and told
a knight who was extremely bold
was entering the land, impelled
to save the queen, who was now held   2120
by Meleagant, the monarch's son.
"I think this knight must be the one,"
he told himself, "so I shall ask."
He said: "Sir, tell me of your task;
do not in any part conceal it,
and in exchange, when you reveal it,

I'll counsel you as I see fit.
Since I shall also benefit
if you perform successfully,
2130   please do reveal the truth to me;
your purposes and mine convene.
I think you came here for the queen
among its treacherous citizens,
far worse than any Saracens;*
that is what brings you to the land."
The knight replied: "You understand
that she is all I came to find,
but where my lady is confined
I am unable to infer.
2140   I do intend to rescue her,
and counsel is my greatest need.
If you can counsel me, proceed."
The vavasor began to say:
"You chose a hard and painful way.
This path is leading you straight toward
the passage called the Bridge of the Sword.
If you heed me and are astute,
you'll take another safer route
to find the Sword Bridge. On your ride
2150   I shall have someone be your guide."
The knight desired the shortest road.
"Is it as straight as that I rode?"
he asked about that other way.
"No," said his host, "but I can say
it is a longer, safer trail."
The knight said: "It's of no avail;
tell me about this pathway to it,
for I am ready to pursue it."
"True, sir, your fame would not be great,
2160   were you to choose the alternate.
Tomorrow you will promptly face
much trouble when you reach a place
called the Stone Passage. Shall I say

how dreadful is this passageway?
One horse alone can cross its crest.
Two men cannot proceed abreast.
The passage is not only hard
but well defended by the guard,
who won't surrender it outright.
The moment that you reach the site   2170
you will receive as your reward
many a blow from lance and sword
and pay back many of your own
before you cross this pass of stone."
After the vavasor was done,
a knight stepped out, who was his son:
"I wish to go on this knight's mission
provided, sir, you give permission."
At that one of the youths arose.
"I shall go with him too," he chose.   2180
The father, with a willing heart,
allowed his two sons to depart.
The knight need not proceed alone
to cross the Passageway of Stone,
and so he thanked them gratefully,
delighted to have company.
When there was no more to be said,
they led the knight to seek his bed
to let him slumber, if he might.
He rose when he could see daylight,   2190
observed at once by those who chose
to go with him, who swiftly rose.
The two knights armed themselves and started.
Upon leavetaking, they departed.
They placed the younger boy ahead
and rode along the way that led
to the Stone Passage, which in time
they reached just at the hour of prime.
Upon the Stony Passageway
there was a battlement midway,   2200

[61]

and on its top there was a man.
Before the group came near the span,
the man atop the structure spied
the riders, and he loudly cried:
"Some enemies have come to fight!"
Immediately a mounted knight
rode out upon the battlement
in armor, new, without a dent,
and on each side were men-at-arms
2210 who had sharp axes in their arms.
But as the passage was approached,
the man who was the watch reproached
the cart knight vilely. He was told:
"Oh, vassal, you were overbold.
You were a fool, naive and grand,
the day you crossed into this land.
No man should travel to these parts
who ever rode around in carts.
May God grant you no joy of it."
2220 Each knight rode toward the opposite
as rapidly as horses may.
The guardian of the passageway
struck with his lance, snapped it in half,
and dropped both pieces of the staff.
The knight took aim above the shield,
the edge that left some throat revealed,
and threw him backward and across
the passage stones with one hard toss.
The axemen leapt but landed blows
2230 that missed the knight, because they chose
to misdirect the blows they aimed,
so knight and horse would not be maimed.
When the knight realized that the armed
axemen were leaving him unharmed,
he did not choose to draw his sword.
Unchallenged by them, he pressed forward
and crossed the passage on his route

with his companions in pursuit.
Each told the other he had never
seen such a knight or such endeavor,   2240
and there was no one as prestigious.
"Is not what he has done prodigious,
to force through to the other side?"
"For Heaven's sake, dear brother, ride,"
the older knight said to the youth,
"and tell my father the whole truth
about this marvellous adventure."
The young man vowed he would not venture
back to their father to recite
the tale; he would not leave this knight   2250
until he earned the accolade
and by him was a knight new-made.
His brother could carry the fantastic
news if he felt enthusiastic.
The three continued on their way
for the remainder of the day.

THE RIOT

PAST none they met a traveller
who asked the three men who they were.
They answered: "We are knights who press
onward about our business."   2260
"Sir, I would like to have you lodge
with me, you and your entourage,"
he told the knight and not the brothers,
as lord and master of the others,
because he seemed to have more power.
"I can't seek shelter at this hour," *
the knight responded straightaway.
"Only a coward would delay
or would repose at ease and rest

[63]

2270 when he has gone on such a quest;
my business is of such a kind,
for hours no lodging would I find."
The traveller made this reply:
"My dwelling place is not nearby
but a good distance on away.
You'd reach it later in the day
and lodge when more appropriate.
When you have come it would be late."
"I shall proceed there without fail."
2280 The party went along the trail.
The man led them toward his abode;
the others followed on the road.
When they had ridden a long distance,
they met a squire full of insistence
who'd galloped there without surcease
upon a nag, round and obese
as an apple, the entire stretch.
He told the man he came to fetch:
"Sir, come at once, we are disquieted.
2290 A host of Logrians has rioted;*
they are at war with everyone.
The war already has begun
as has the combat, strife, and fight,
and furthermore, they say a knight,
one who has fought in many places,
is in our country. In all cases
no one could stop him with a blow
from going where he wants to go;
a knight whom no one can withstand.
2300 All prisoners within this land
say he will soon grant them remission
and force our people to submission.
Now hurry on, sir, as I said."
The man went galloping ahead.
The rest were joyful at the news;
they also heard it and would choose

to help their own men in the battle.
"Sir, listen to this armed man's prattle,"
declared the son of the vavasor.
"Let's help our people in their war   2310
against the natives of this place."
Their guide was traveling apace.
Not waiting for them, he rode fast
on toward a fortress, which stood fast
upon a hill, and sped away
until he reached the entryway.
The three spurred after him and chased.
A high wall and a moat encased
the bailey, wholly isolated.
As soon as they had penetrated,*   2320
upon their heels a gate was dropped,
so the invaders could be stopped
from riding out the way they came.
"Come, come," they started to exclaim,
"now this is no place to abide,"
and hastened to pursue the guide
into a passage that extended
before the riders undefended,
but when the guide had ridden through,
another sliding doorway flew   2330
in place as it was dropped behind.
The riders were distressed to find
they were enclosed by door and wall,
for they believed that one and all
had been enchanted by a spell.
The knight of whom I've more to tell
possessed and wore a finger ring.*
Such power was it harboring,
enchantments would be overthrown
once he had gazed upon the stone.   2340
He put the ring before his eyes,
gazed at the stone, and said likewise:
"So help me Heaven, Lady, Lady,

[65]

I have great need of you to aid me."
This lady was a fairy being,
and she had given him the ring
and nurtured him in infancy.
He trusted her ability,
in any place that harm waylaid him,
2350　to bring him help and come to aid him,
but his appeal had clearly shown,
as had the fairy ring and stone,
that no enchantment had arisen.
They were enclosed within their prison.
The raiders started to explore
until they reached a well-barred door
of a low, narrow postern gate
that they had managed to locate.
They drew their swords and struck it hard;
2360　the beam snapped, and it was unbarred.
Outside the tower the view revealed
the wild, fierce fight down in the field.
When they excluded crowds of peasants,
they saw that they were in the presence
of easily a thousand knights
on either side, engaged in fights.
When they went down onto the plain,
the vavasor's son spoke again,
and he was prudent and judicious:
2370　"I think, sir, it would be propitious
for us to ask, before we go
to seek the battlefield below,
upon which side our people are.
I do not know from where they war,
but if you wish, I shall inquire."
The knight replied: "I so desire.
Be quick and come back right away."
The son went down to view the fray
and in a short time he returned.
2380　"We're fortunate, for I have learned

[66]

our people fight upon this side;
I saw that clearly," he replied.
The knight went hastening toward the fight.
He met with an approaching knight
and struck so hard in eye and head,
his foe collapsed and fell down dead.
The younger son got to the ground,
and seized the horse and arms he found,
which were the knight's before the kill,
and armed himself with speed and skill.   2390
When he was armored for the field,
he mounted, and he seized the shield
and painted lance, stout and unbending,
with which the knight had been contending,
and flashing blade with which he vied,
and he attached them to his side.
He joined the fray with lance and sword
after his brother and his lord,
who for some time had been acquitting
himself well, shattering and splitting   2400
the lances, shields, and hauberk mail.
Iron and wood could not prevail
against the mighty blows he hacked
or shield the men whom he attacked.
He knocked some off their chargers, dead.
Alone he proved so talented
that all his foes in combat fell
and his companions battled well.
The men from Logres were amazed
they did not know him; several raised   2410
the matter with the vavasor's son.
He told them: "Lords, he is the one
who has arrived to set us free
from exile and adversity,
which all of us have long endured.
So our release could be procured,
the knight has passed through many places,

with perils laden in some cases,
and he will pass through many more.
2420 He's done much and has much in store;
so we must honor and revere him."
Then everyone rejoiced to hear him,
when this news spread to everyone.
They heard and knew what he had done
and what it meant to them at length.
The joy they felt increased their strength.
They were emboldened to oppose
and slaughter many of their foes,
and they abused them in this fight,
2430 more on account of that one knight,
that single knight, or so I find,
than all the other knights combined.
Had it not been so close to night,
they would have put their foes to flight,
but night, dark night, came on so fast,
it forced them to depart at last.
When they departed from the plain,
the captives all, as if in pain,
came at the knight from every side,
2440 and seized him by the rein, and cried:
"Welcome to you, noble sir!"
Then up spoke every follower:
"Stay with me, by the faith I claim,
my lord, by God and by His name,
please stay with me and only me."
So spoke the young and elderly,
for one and all they felt compelled
to give him lodging where they dwelled,
and each one said: "You would prefer
2450 my lodgings to another's, sir."
Each gathered round him to belabor
the point and steal him from his neighbor.
Their every home they did propose
and very nearly came to blows,

for each one wished to give him housing.
He said it was a foolish, rousing,
but idle subject of dissention.
"Stop all this wrangling and contention,
which neither you or I can need.
We ought not to have disagreed   2460
among ourselves, I have no doubt;
we ought to help each other out.
My lodgings should not make you brawl,
but, for the benefit of all,
instead you ought to take good care
to find me lodgings someplace where
I am directly on my route."
At once they started to dispute:
"At my house, then!" "No, at my own!"
The knight said: "Still no better tone;   2470
such quarrels merit ridicule.
I think your wisest man a fool
to hear the arguments you say.
You ought to speed me on my way;
instead you want me to detour.
If you had managed to procure,
in order, gladly, one by one,
whatever honors may be done
to one man in another's home,
by all the saints revered in Rome,   2480
I'd not feel more appreciative,
while taking all you have to give,
than I feel at the thought you want me.
Great joy and health may Heaven grant me;
my pleasure in what you intended
is just as if you had extended
your kindliness in vast amounts,
so let it be the thought that counts."
He won them over in this way.
They took him down the road to stay   2490
with an extremely well-off knight,

[69]

all serving him as best they might.
Great pains and effort were employed;
they did him honor, overjoyed,
all evening till bedtime drew near,
because they held him very dear.
Next morning, when he left, the throng
sought eagerly to go along.
Each man proposed his fellowship.
2500 The knight refused: upon this trip
there was no man he sought with him
except the two he brought with him.
He took them with him but no others.

THE PROUD KNIGHT

UPON that day the knight and brothers
rode on from morn until eventide
with no adventures on their ride.
Their horses at a rapid gait,
they came out of a forest late.
When they emerged they saw a house
2510 owned by a knight, and saw his spouse,
who seemed like a superior
fine lady seated at the door.
The lady sprang up from her place
with a delighted, joyous face,
once she saw them, and came to meet them.
"Be welcome," she began to greet them,
"and I should like to have you stay.
You have a lodging place today;
dismount," the lady told the band.
2520 "My lady, since it's your command,
thank you; tonight we shall descend
and take the lodging you extend."
Once that the riders had descended,

the lady had the horses tended.
Her household was well trained and drilled.
She called her sons and daughters: skilled
young men, polite and dutiful,
knights, daughters who were beautiful,
who came as soon as they could come.
The lady promptly ordered some   2530
to take the saddle off each steed
and groom it well. They all agreed;
no one would dare refuse outright.
She asked them to disarm each knight.
The daughters leapt up to divest them
of armor hastily, and dressed them
in short cloaks brought for them to wear.
Their lodging place was very fair;
they led the riders in at once.
The lord, accompanied by two sons,   2540
was not within the dwelling place
but occupied still with the chase.
His homecoming was not belated.
His household was well regulated
and leapt to meet him at the door.
They took the venison he bore,
which they unloaded and untied.
"Sir, sir, you do not know," they cried.
"Some knights have come to be our guests."
The lord responded, "God be blessed."   2550
And so the two sons and the knight
welcomed their guests with great delight.
The household did not seem unflurried,
for even its least members hurried
to do whatever might be needed.
Some ran to have the dinner speeded,
some to fetch many candlesticks,
so light glowed from the burning wicks,
and other persons went to hasten
and offer water, towel, and basin   2560

[71]

to every member, guest, and lord.
They were unsparing as they poured.
All washed their hands and then were seated,
and thereabouts no eye was greeted
by anything that seemed unpleasant.
With the first course there came a present:
a knight arrived outside the door
upon a charger. He was more
proud in his manner than a bull,
2570   a beast whose pride is plentiful.
The knight was armed from head to foot,
one foot in stirrup, one foot put,
so he would seem smart and urbane,
over his charger's flowing mane.
The proud knight gave himself such airs
and came upon them unawares.
Nobody noticed till he came
before them with these words of blame:
"I want to know whose head contains
2580   a vacuum in the place of brains,
who is so arrogant and dumb
as to be in this country, come
to cross the Sword Bridge? He is tiring
himself for nothing by aspiring;
his footsteps were a total loss."
"I am the one who means to cross,"
the knight, without the slightest qualm,
responded with the utmost calm.
"You? You? How dare you think it ever?
2590   Before you chose such an endeavor
and thought of doing such a deed,
I think you should have given heed
to what the outcome might entail
and have remembered without fail
that cart in which you were paraded.
I don't know if you feel degraded
by mounting it at such expense,

but nobody with any sense
would take on such an obligation
after such deep humiliation."   2600
He did not deign to say one word
in answer to what he had heard.
Of course the master of the house,
his household, children, and his spouse
were much astonished by this speech.
"What great misfortune, God!" said each.
"The hour when a cart was first
planned and constructed be accursed;
it is pernicious and malign
in its invention and design.   2610
Oh, God above! Why was he carted?
What accusations were imparted?
What was his sin? What was his crime?
He has been sentenced for all time.
If he were rid of this disgrace,
while the wide world remains in place
no knight would be found, none alone,
whatever prowess had he shown,
like him, one no knight has resembled.
If all the knights could be assembled,   2620
to tell the truth, none would be seen
with such a handsome, noble mien."
The people spoke in unison.
The proud knight had again begun
to utter words that were untoward:
"Hark, knight who seeks the Bridge of the Sword,*
instead of crossing you can float.
I'll have you carried in a boat
across the water, swift and light,
if you prefer, but then I might   2630
decide to charge you for the ride
once we are on the other side:
the fee's your head, no controversy,
or else it shall be at my mercy."

[exemplifieo how truly awful it is to be in a cart]

[73]

The knight said he did not endeavor
to seek misfortune and would never
let his own head be risked or lost,
whatever happened when he crossed.
The other knight pursued his theme.
2640   "Since you will not accept my scheme,
whatever may be the shame or woe,
in that case you will have to go
outside and fight me man to man."
After he had announced this plan,
the knight replied, to be amusing:
"If there were some way of refusing,
I would avoid it willingly,
but then I might as well agree.
To fighting I am less averse
2650   than waiting here for something worse."
Before the knight rose from the table,
as rapidly as they were able
he told the youths who served that course
to put the saddle on his horse
and fetch the arms that he would need.
They strove to do his will with speed.
To one his arms were paramount;
another ran to fetch his mount.
When he rode off with all his arms,
2660   his shield held fast by the enarmes,
upon his charger, firmly mounted,
it seemed as though he should be counted
among the fair and good and pure,
of that you may be very sure.
So willing was the charger shown
that it appeared to be his own,
as was the shield that he held fast;
through the shield straps his arm was passed.
Upon his head his helm was laced,
2670   and it was so correctly placed,
you'd not have thought it had been lent.

[74]

You would have been so well content
with his equipment, you'd have said
the knight must have been born and bred
to the equipment he received,
and I should like to be believed.
The knight who sought the joust, cocksure,
was past the gate out on a moor
whereon the battle would take place.
Each spurred on at a rapid pace   2680
when his foe reached his field of vision,
came into violent collision,
and gave each other such a blow,
each lance began to bend and bow,
and both their lances flew to bits.
They used their swords to score such hits
on shields and helms and hauberk mail,
they split the wood, broke iron scale,
with so much anger in those cases,
they hurt themselves in several places.   2690
They traded blows when they attacked
like dealers honoring a pact,
so bloodthirsty that they would stoop
to slip swords on a horse's croup
and even strike a horse's side,
until both mounts collapsed and died.*
The two knights, when they had been put
upon the ground and were on foot,
sought one another out to duel
to death and could not be more cruel   2700
about their sword play or preciser.
Their blows fell faster than a dicer
with shillings at a risk of loss
doubling his bets at every toss,
and yet this game of theirs evolved
elsewise; there were no dice involved,
but hard blows and a fight so horrible,
that it was vicious and deplorable.

[75]

The sight of it was so compelling,
2710   everyone came outside the dwelling.
The lord, the lady, daughter, son—
the battle was ignored by none—
household member or merely viewer,
they all lined up upon the moor,
which was extremely broad and wide,
to watch the warriors as they vied.
When they appeared, the knight of the cart
swore he had played a coward's part
to see his host was watching there,
2720   and slowly he became aware
the others watched him, all assembled.
In fury, his whole body trembled,
for he considered long ago
he should have overcome his foe
and should have managed to defeat him.
The knight struck at his foe and beat him
with the sword, near his head and fast,
then came upon him like a blast
and pushed him back without remission,
2730   until he took his foe's position
and drove him back till he rescinded
more ground, and was completely winded,
and left himself more unprotected.
The knight at that point recollected
how shamefully his foe reproached
the cart that he had once approached
and felt such rage when he attacked,
no strap or lacing stayed intact
around the neckband as he slashed.
2740   The helmet flew off as he bashed;
the ventail fell beneath a blow.
He kept belaboring his foe
and made him sue for mercy like
the lark before the merlin's strike,*
who has no place she can seek cover,

[76]

because the merlin flies above her
and can surpass her in a race.
The challenger in sheer disgrace
came up to ask for clemency
because there was no remedy.   2750
Once that the knight heard that he pled,
he did not touch or strike, instead,
"Want mercy?" asked the knight of the cart.
His foe responded: "Aren't you smart,"
continuing his ridicule.
"You've spoken like an utter fool.
There's nothing that you could endow
I want as much as mercy now."
The knight said: "In a cart you'll mount.
Your words will be of no account,   2760
for you have such a foolish tongue,
with those vile insults that you flung,
unless you mount the cart and ride."
"Please God," the losing knight replied,
"I'll never mount the cart, not I."
"No?" said the knight, "then you will die."
"Sir, do whatever pleases you.
By God, I beg you, and I sue
for mercy, and with my whole heart,
but do not make me mount the cart.   2770
I will bear any punishments
but that one, which is so immense.
I think I would prefer to face
one hundred deaths than such disgrace.
Besides the cart, there is no task
too arduous that you could ask,
so that I can win clemency
and your consent to pardon me."
While he endeavored to secure
a pardon, from across the moor   2780
a maid* arrived without preamble
upon a tawny mule at amble.

[77]

She was disheveled and uncloaked
and held a whip with which she stroked
the mule with many a blow and wallop.
No charger, paced at a great gallop,
to tell the truth of it, could scramble
as swiftly as that mule could amble.
The maid said to the knight of the cart:
2790 "God grant you joy within your heart
from someone who delights you best."
The knight heard and did not protest,
"You also, maid; may Heaven bless
and grant you health and happiness."
On hearing his reply in kind
the maiden chose to speak her mind.
"Knight, I have come from far away
and have great need of you today.
I ask a favor and a boon.
2800 I'll make as great and opportune
a recompense as I can manage,
and it will be to your advantage.
I think you'll come to need my aid."
The knight responded: "Tell me, maid,
what boon you seek, and if I may,
it shall be yours without delay,
if it is not too hard to grant."
She said: "It is the head I want
of him you conquered in this fight.
2810 In truth, you'll never find a knight
as treacherous and despicable.
You'd not be sinning, doing ill,
but charity, by so agreeing.
He is the most disloyal being
that ever was or is to come."
The warrior who was overcome
could hear she sought to see him dead,
"Do not believe this maid," he said,
"she hates me, but have mercy, rather,

[78]

by God who is both son and father⋆   2820
and who in turn His mother made
of His own daughter and handmaid."
The maid's contempt was all the greater.
"Ha! Knight, do not believe this traitor.
God grant you honor, joy, and fame
as great as you may care to claim,
and grant you a successful ending
to the endeavor you have pending."
The knight was now so tightly caught
that for some time he paused and thought.   2830
Should he bestow the head, he wondered,
on one who urged that it be sundered,
or did he care so for the knight
he would take pity on his plight?
He wished to please both knight and maid,
the way Largess and Mercy bade,
for these two virtues gave commands   *Like and love Reason*
that he comply with their demands.
Both generous and merciful,
he was responsive to their pull.   2840
If the maid took away the head,
then Mercy would be crushed and dead.
Did she not carry it away,
Largess would surely lose the day.
Therefore both Mercy and Largess
had him in prison in distress,
and each tormented him and pricked him
about the head of his knight victim.
The maid who sought it would prefer
that he bestow the head on her;   2850
the knight sought mercy for his part,
appealing to his noble heart.
Since he has begged for clemency,
ought not the other to agree?
Indeed, he never could resist
even his worst antagonist,

[79]

Grants mercy
1st time but
never a
second

once he was utterly defeated,
and begged for mercy, and entreated.
He granted mercy at this price:

2860   he pardoned once but never twice.
He should have mercy on his foe,
as was his custom to bestow,
as the knight begged of him and pled.
What of the maid who wants his head;
is she to have it? Yes, she can.
"Knight," he responded, "man to man
we'll fight again immediately.
I'll show you this much clemency,
since you are seeking a reprieve:

2870   I shall allow you to retrieve
your helmet and to do your best
to arm your frame and head unpressed.
But be aware that you will die
if you are conquered on this try."
The knight replied: "I ask no more.
No clemency shall I implore
apart from that you are extending."
"Moreover, when we are contending,
so you may have the upper hand,

2880   I shall not move from where I stand."
The knight, rearming in a hurry,
resumed the dueling with fury,

lost
again

but swiftly he was at the worst.
His foe, as he had done at first,
defeated him with greater ease.
At once the maid resumed her pleas:
"Knight, do not spare his life anew,
no matter what he says to you.
He would not have spared you, for sure,

2890   had he once been your conqueror,
and you must know and must believe
that he means only to deceive;
he'll hoodwink you immediately.

[80]

Good knight, do give his head to me.
Behead the most disloyal man
within the realm and empire's span.
You ought to make me this donation;
I'll give you lavish compensation
in days to come when I repay you,
but if he can he will betray you   2900
another time by words and breath."
The one who saw approaching death
cried out for mercy long and loud,
and yet his cries were disallowed
with all the arguments he gasped.
The knight immediately grasped
his helmet, managing to sever
the lacing thongs by his endeavor,
and then he knocked his ventail off,
together with his shining coif.   2910
The swiftest plea his foe could make
was: "Mercy, vassal, for God's sake!"
The knight replied: "To save my soul,
I shall not pity or condole
with you I spared at the beginning."
"Oh," he exclaimed, "You would be sinning,
if you believe my enemy
and in this manner murder me."
To one side she who sought his death
exhorted him in the same breath   2920
to hurry and cut off his head
and not believe a word he said.
The knight's sword struck him hard and sure;
the head flew off upon the moor;
to earth the severed body fell,
which greatly pleased the demoiselle.
He picked the head up by the hair
and placed it in the maiden's care.
"Whatever is your heart's desire,
I truly hope it may inspire   2930

[81]

such joy as my heart feels, elated
about the person I most hated.
I don't feel any sense of wrong
except that he survived so long.
Rely upon me for a boon
whenever it is opportune.
This service to me, I've foresaid it,
will turn out greatly to your credit.
Now I shall go, and I commend you
2940 to God, and pray He may defend you."
They left each other in God's grace;
the maiden quickly left the place.
All those upon the moor who'd viewed
the battle felt joy unsubdued.
Rejoicing, they disarmed the knight
and honored him as best they might.
At once they started to repeat
their handwashing so they could eat.
They sat down to their meal and dined
2950 in a far better frame of mind
than they were customarily.
When they'd dined long and merrily,
the vavasor turned and addressed
this statement to his seated guest:
"My lord, some time ago we came
from Logres, realm that we can claim
by birth; so we extend our wishes
you will be honored, have great riches,
and find great joy within this spot,
2960 for we shall also share your lot,
and many more will benefit
if honor, wealth, and perquisite
befall you in this land and way."
He said, "May God hear what you say."

another term for vassal [handwritten annotation]

THE SWORD BRIDGE

ONCE that the vavasor had stopped,
his words had ceased, his voice had dropped,
a son of his made this proposal:
"Sir, we shall place at your disposal
all our possessions and resources
and give you aid and not discourses,   2970
for you will need them in your task.
We should not wait for you to ask.
Sir, do not be discomforted
because your steed has fallen dead.
Here we have chargers full of powers.
Please take as many as are ours,
whatever you desire and need,
the best ones, to replace your steed,
for you will need them on your ride."
"Most willingly," the knight replied.   2980
They had beds made and sought repose.
Next morning, early, they arose
and were equipped to make their start.
When they were ready to depart,
they took their leave, the knight and brothers,
of the lord, lady, and all others,
and courteously sought their permission.
So that there will be no omission,
I'll say the knight was not content
to mount the charger that was lent   2990
and offered to him at the door,
so I shall tell you one thing more:
He chose to have one of the pair
of knights accompanying him there
accept the horse he had been loaned.
He took the charger that knight owned,
which met and suited his own needs.
When all the knights were on their steeds,

[83]

the three of them left on their mission
3000 with their host's leave and his permission,
for he had done his very best
to serve and honor every guest.
They rode the path that did not wind,
till gradually the day declined,
and reached the Sword Bridge, which appeared
when none was past and vespers neared.
At the foot of this appalling span
the knights dismounted. Every man
could see the treacherous water swirling,
3010 black and rushing, thick and curling,
and vile enough to cause a shiver,
as if it were the Devil's river,
so dangerous and swift and deep,
whatever fell within its sweep
the world round might as well be tossed
into an icy sea and lost.
The bridge was fashioned differently
from all that were or are to be.
There never was, may I be frank,
3020 so vile a bridge or vile a plank.
It was a polished, shining sword
beneath which icy water poured,
but this sword bridge was stiff and strong
and built to be two lances long.*
On each side were great tree trunks, matched,
to which the sword blade was attached.
Nobody feared a fall impending,
caused by its shattering or bending:
the bridge appeared in such a state
3030 that it would bear a heavy weight.
The two knights who were with the third
were much upset, for they concurred
there were two lions or leopards* tied
to a large boulder on the side
across the Sword Bridge, they believed,

[84]

if their own eyes were not deceived.
The lions, bridge, and murky stream
were chilling to such an extreme
the terror of it made them quake.
They told the knight: "My lord, do take   3040
advice about this sight and heed it,
for you will find that you will need it.
This bridge is hideously erected,
ill-fashioned, awkwardly connected.
If you do not repent, and soon,*
you will sometime inopportune
and realize that you were mistaken.
Some things should not be undertaken
except with cautiousness and care.
Suppose you did cross over there   3050
—it's an impossible event,
as there is no way to prevent
the winds from blowing or contain them,
and birds: nobody can restrain them
so that they dare no longer sing,
nor can a man be entering
his mother's womb for his rebirth;
these things all cannot be on earth
no more than emptying the sea—
but if you do cross, don't you see   3060
that those two lions, fierce and savage,
are waiting over there to ravage
and kill you, fastened in their chains,
and suck the life blood from your veins,
and eat your flesh, within their maw,
down to the bones, which they will gnaw?
I don't see how I have the nerve
to watch the lions and observe.
They'll kill you, if you don't take care;
soon they will start to break and tear   3070
your limbs away out of your body,
no mercy shown to anybody.

You ought not to be so severe.
Take pity on yourself, stay here.
you only will debase yourself
if, wittingly, you place yourself
in certain danger you will die."
The knight said, laughing, in reply:
"My lords, I do appreciate
3080 your deep concern about my fate;
it demonstrates sincere affection.
I know you have no predilection
toward seeing me thus come to grief,
but I have such faith, such belief
that through all God will be my guard,
I don't feel any more regard
for bridge and water than hard ground.
On the adventure I am bound
the crossing is my next concern.
3090 Better to die than to return."
They had no choice but to accept.
In pity both knights sighed and wept.
Thereon the knight prepared himself
as best he could to cross the gulf.
He did a strange and wondrous feat,
for he disarmed his hands and feet.
They would not be in good condition
when he attained, upon his mission,
the other bank but would afford
3100 a firmer grip upon the sword,
for it was sharper than a scythe.
So he decided to rely
on hands and feet bared and not use
his leggings, uppers, or his shoes.
He did not feel intimidated
if feet and hands were lacerated.
He'd rather cross the Sword Bridge maimed
than tumble off it and be claimed
by waters where he would submerge,

from which he never could emerge. 3110
With greatest agony in store
he crossed the bridge. His pain was sore;
hands, knees, and feet were cut and bleeding,
but Love, while guiding him and leading,
consoled him, so his pains were sweet.
He used his hands and knees and feet,
and crawled across the narrow plank
until he reached the other bank.
Then he recalled the lion pair
he thought he'd seen from over there 3120
and looked about him, but he found
not one small lizard on the ground
or anything to cause him harm.
To check his ring for spell or charm,
he raised his hand before his face.
With neither lion at that place,
which he was sure he had perceived,
he thought himself charmed and deceived.
No living thing was near the plank.
The knights upon the other bank 3130
rejoiced to see that he had crossed
but did not realize the cost
in terms of injury and pain.
He thought it greatly to his gain
he'd not endured worse injuries.
He wiped his wounds with his chemise
so the compression staunched the blood.
Before him a strong tower stood;
it was so strong that it surpassed
all towers he'd sighted in the past; 3140
it could not have displayed more skill.
Leaning on a window sill
therein was King Bademagu,
a ruler diligent and true
whose sense of honor was acute.
In all he was of high repute,

and noted for his loyalty.
His son would do the contrary
whenever he could find a reason,
3150 because he was so full of treason.
The son, one never tired or bored
by treachery or vice, abhorred
behavior, any cruel thing,
leaned out the window by the king.
While they were watching from this height,
across the Sword Bridge crawled the knight,
although it hurt him viciously.
Meleagant flushed maliciously,
because he knew, with rage and spleen,
3160 he would be challenged for the queen,
yet as a knight he was the kind
who feared no man, however inclined,
however bold or boisterous.
Were he not cruel and treacherous,
he would have had no counterpart,
and yet he had a wooden heart
of kindness totally devoid.
The king was pleased and overjoyed;
his son found it a painful sight.
3170 The king was certain that the knight
who crawled across the Sword-Bridge span
was unsurpassed by any man,
for none would dare cross at that place
if he had in him any trace
of Cowardice, which shames its own
far more than Prowess fames its own,
for Prowess can accomplish less
than Cowardice and Laziness.
In truth, let it be undersood:
3180 it's easier to do harm than good.
Of these two things I've more to say,
except that it creates delay,
so I shall focus on the serial

[88]

and shall return to my material.
Now I'll relate to everyone
the father's lecture to his son.
"It was by chance, son, that we came
and leaned out of this window frame,
but we were very well rewarded,
because thereby we were afforded   3190
a view of the most bold attempt
that ever has been done or dreamt.
Tell me, do you not feel regard
for one who did a deed so hard
that it was wondrous to be seen?
Reach an accord; return the queen.
Set no conditions; give her back.
You'll win no fame if you attack
and might sustain great injury.
Show wisdom now and courtesy;   3200
send him the queen, as is his due,
before he comes to look for you.
Do him this honor in your land:
before the knight makes his demand,
give him the one he came to find,
for you must surely bear in mind
he's searching for Queen Guinevere.
You must not let yourself appear
proud, stubborn, foolish, overblown.
If he is in your land alone,   3210
you ought to keep him company.
A gentleman should graciously
give one such, of his welcome, proof
and ought not to remain aloof.
Who honors another, honor accrues.*
You will be honored, if you choose
to do him honor and to serve
this man who is, as we observe,
the best knight in the world around him."
Said Meleagant: "May God confound him,   3220

[89]

if there's none better or as good."
His father erred in parenthood
when he neglected Meleagant.
It made him no less arrogant.
He said: "Shall I join feet and hands
and as his vassal hold my lands?
I'll be his liege man, ranking mean,

3228 before I give him back the queen!
3228a The queen! May God above forbid★
3228b I yield her just because I'm bid!
So help me God, I won't surrender,
3230 but I shall challenge and defend her
against each fool and blunderer
who dares to come in search of her!"
The king replied immediately:
"Son, it would be a courtesy
if your great stubbornness would cease.
I warn and urge you to make peace.
You know what honors will accrue★
if he can win the queen from you
in combat on the battlefield.

3240 He'd rather fight and make you yield
the queen than have her be presented,
because his fame will be augmented.
Now I believe he has no use
for reacquiring her by truce;
he wants to win the queen by might.
Be wise, deprive him of the fight.
I warn and urge you to make peace;
I am distressed by your caprice.★
If my advice leaves you averse,

3250 I shan't care if you are the worse,
and great misfortune may befall.
This knight need fear no one at all
except for you and you alone.
For all my men and on my own
I offer truce and surety.

I've not committed treachery
or any felony or treason
and shall not start for any reason,
for you or foreigners, no matter.
You know I never mean to flatter.   3260
Whatever this foreign knight may need:
new arms and armor or a steed,
they shall be his at my insistence
since he has boldly come this distance.
His liberty shall be respected;
he shall be thoroughly protected
from all but you and you alone.
I warn you, if this man is shown
to save himself from you, my son,
then he need not fear anyone."   3270
"I've time to listen at my leisure,
and you may say what gives you pleasure,"
said Meleagant, "while I keep silent,
but I have not become compliant
or found your arguments conclusive.
By nature I am not reclusive
or noble, kind, or charitable,
nor will I be so honorable
and give him her whom I love best.
The knight will not fulfill his quest   3280
as soon as you and he surmise.
It will be wholly otherwise.
If you assist him and prefer
his side to mine, we won't concur.
What's it to me, and what's the use
if he enjoys a peace and truce
with you and every other male?
It will not cause my heart to fail.
My pleasure is extraordinary
that I am his sole adversary,   3290
and furthermore, by God my Savior,
I have not asked you any favor

[91]

involving any treacheries.
You be as noble as you please,
and you can leave me to be cruel."
"What? Will you not decline to duel?"
"No." "Then I have no more to say.
Do your best, while I make my way
downstairs to talk with that bold knight,
3300 and I shall offer him outright
whatever help I can provide,
for I am wholly on his side."
The king left after this discourse
and had them saddle up his horse.
They brought out an enormous mount.
He used the stirrup ring to mount
and took some of his men, but few:
three knights, and men-at-arms but two.
The group proceeded down the bank,
3310 until they rode down to the plank
and saw the man who staunched his slashes
and wiped the red blood from his gashes.
The king thought he would be his guest
for a long time to heal and rest,
but he might just as easily
have thought he could dry up the sea.
The king rode toward the bridge with speed,
where he dismounted from his steed.
The wounded man stood up to greet him,
3320 not knowing who had come to meet him.
Although the knight had to withstand
acute pain in both foot and hand,
he kept his suffering concealed,
as if he were completely healed.
The king saw him collect his forces
and ran to offer his resources.
He greeted him: "Sir, to be candid,
I am amazed that you have landed
upon us in the way you came,

but you are welcome all the same. 3330
No one thus entered our domain,
and no one ever will again.
We shall not find so bold a stranger
who'll put himself in such great danger.
I like you more for this attempt.
You've done what no one else has dreamt,
and you will find me very cordial,
extremely courteous, and loyal.
I am the ruler of this land,
and I shall place at your command 3340
whatever help I can extend
and any counsel I can lend.
Now I can easily perceive
why you have come: I do believe
that you have come to seek the queen."
"Sire," he replied, "as you have seen,
I came here to no other end."
"But you must spare no pains, my friend,
before she's yours," the ruler stated,
"and you are badly lacerated. 3350
The injuries and blood are clear.
As for the one who brought you here,
you will not find him so forthright
he'll yield the queen without a fight.
But you must have your gashes treated
until their healing is completed;
the ointment of the Marys three,★
and better ointments, if there be,
I'll give for their alleviation
to hasten your recuperation, 3360
for that is foremost in my mind.
The queen is carefully confined,★
and no man troubles her with lust.
My son considers it unjust,
because he led her off with him.
No man could be as crazed and grim;

[93]

his frenzied rage is unsubdued,
but I am in a cordial mood,
so help me Heaven, and desire

3370 to give you all that you require.
However good his arms may be,
though he will be displeased with me,
arms just as good I shall concede
together with the horse you need.
I grant you absolute protection,
no matter who may raise objection,
and there is no one you need fear
save him who brought the queen back here.
No man has threatened anyone

3380 as sternly as I did my son.
I almost drove him from my land
in wrath that he refused to hand
the queen to you when first you came;
he is my son, but all the same,
don't be concerned by any tattle:
unless he conquers you in battle,
he cannot do you any ill
or any harm against my will."
"I thank you, sire," replied the knight.

3390 "The time I'm wasting at this site
I would not lose and cannot spare.
Since nothing hurts me anywhere,
no wounds I have sustained feel sore,
just lead me to this warrior,
for with such weapons as I carry
I am prepared to deal and parry
and to receive blows and contend."
"You would do best to wait, my friend,
for two or three full weeks of rest,

3400 until your injuries are dressed
and given time to heal and close.
You need at least two week's repose.
Then, I could never let you fight

—I could not even bear the sight—
with the accoutrement before me,
however much you may implore me."
The knight responded: "If you please,
I'll use no other arms but these
I'll gladly carry in the fray,
nor do I seek the least delay,   3410
not one hour, not a single moment
of rest, or respite, or postponement.
The sole concession I shall make
is waiting till dawn for your sake,
but I shall brook no more delay
for anything that people say."
The ruler gave the knight his word
it all would be as he preferred
and had him taken to his rooms.
The monarch told the knights and grooms   3420
who led him there to serve his guest.
His escorts did their very best.
The king, who would have been relieved
if only peace could be achieved,
went riding back to find his son
and talk with him again as one
whom peace and concord would reward.
"Dear son, please come to an accord.
Don't fight this knight within my court.
He has not ridden here for sport,   3430
to hunt with bows, to search for game,
but for increased renown and fame.
Pursuit of honor is his quest,
and yet he is in need of rest,
as I immediately recognized.
If he had done as I advised,
he'd not be bent on making war
for one month and another more,
yet he's already very keen.
Suppose you give him back the queen,   3440

[95]

do you believe you will be shamed?
Don't fear it, you will not be blamed,
for it is sinful to withhold
something you have no right to hold.
This warrior was prepared to start
the fight at once, with willing heart,
and yet his hands and feet are split,
and slashed, and wounded, and unfit."
"How foolish to make such a bother,"
3450   said Meleagant to his own father.
"Not by the faith I owe Saint Peter
will I heed you as an entreater.
Let horses tear me into pieces,
if I agree to any peaces
or heed your words in this affair.
If he seeks honor, that's my care.
If he seeks fame, that is my right,
and if he wants to start a fight,
I am a hundred times more ready."
3460   "I see your mind has grown unsteady;
this folly shall be yours at length.
Tomorrow you may test your strength
against this knight, whenever you want."
"May no worse fate," said Meleagant,
"ever befall me than that fray!
I wish it could be held today
instead of waiting till tomorrow.
See how my eyes are filled with sorrow.
My face is long—see how it fell—
3470   I'm more downcast than I can tell.
Until I fight and can employ
my weapons, I shall feel no joy;
there will be nothing that can ease me,
or that can comfort me and please me."

THE DUEL FOR THE QUEEN

THE king knew it of no avail;
advice and prayer would only fail,
and so he left his son perforce
and sent a very strong, good horse
and fine arms in the citadel
to one he knew would use them well.   3480
A surgeon* found in that redoubt,
a pious Christian and devout,
and none more loyal on the earth,
whose healing lore was of more worth
than all Montpellier contained,*
because the king had so ordained,
did everything throughout that night
within his skill to heal the knight.
Each knight and maiden, baron, dame
had heard the news, because his fame   3490
spread through the land with much assistance;
they travelled for a long day's distance
throughout the country, all around,
and people who were castle bound,
both foreigners and native-born,
rode hard all night until the morn.
The two groups, at the daybreak hour,
formed such a crowd around the tower
in hopes to see what was afoot,
no one had room to move a foot.   3500
The king rose early from his rest;
the battle left him much distressed.
He went to see his son in haste.
Upon his head his helm was laced,
and it was made in Poitiers.
The king could win no more delay,
nor could he bring about a truce;
although he tried, it was no use.

[97]

Before the tower in mid-square,
3510 with all the people gathered there,
the two knights would be battling,
as willed and ordered by the king.
The king sent for the foreign knight
when it was early morning light
and led him to the tower square;
the Logrians were everywhere.
The way that it is customary
for people near a monastery
to go to church so they can hear
3520 the organs at the feasts each year,
at Pentecost or Christmas Day,
so everyone, in that same way,
assembled in a mighty band.
All foreign maids from Arthur's land
had fasted three days, gone unshod,
and worn hair shirts in hopes that God
would give the knight from Arthur's realm
the strength and nerve to overwhelm
his adversary in this fight
3530 and save the captives from their plight;
they prayed that God would grant him aid.
The natives of the country prayed
likewise that Heaven would accord
the victory to their own lord.
In early morning, in good time,
before the bells had rung for prime,
they led the two men in the square
completely armed upon a pair
of iron-clad horses. Meleagant
3540 seemed nobly born and elegant,
with well-formed arms and legs and feet
appropriate to an athlete.
He wore a helmet and a shield
around his neck that much appealed
and made him an attractive sight,

but all preferred the other knight;
none wished to see this knight disgraced;
all said he totally effaced
Meleagant, who could not compare.
Once the two knights were in the square,   3550
the king arrived and did his best
to stop the battle, and he pressed
to have a peace and truce effected.
His son, though, could not be deflected.
Eventually the ruler ceased
and told them, "Curb your mounts, at least,
till I am at the tower's top.
It's none too kind of you to stop
until I mount the tower stair."
In great distress he left the square   3560
and went directly to the queen,
because she wished to view the scene
and asked of him, the previous night,
to be where she could watch the fight;
The king had readily conceded
this favor to her and proceeded
to lead the queen high in the tower.
He sought to do all in his power
to honor her, and for her placement
he put her at one window casement   3570
and sought another at her right
from which he leaned to watch the sight.
Various people gathered there:
some knights watched with the royal pair,
and gracious ladies were at hand,
and maidens born within that land,
and many captives were about,
in prayer, attentive and devout.
All prisoners, female and male,
who prayed their lord would never fail,   3580
relied on God and on his lance
for aid and for deliverance.

Without delay the two knights vied.
They shoved the people to the side,
elbowed their shields, and slipped their arms
through the thick straps of the enarmes,
and spurred until their lances battered
two arms-lengths through the shields and shattered,
and when they splintered on their marks,
3590 the pieces flew away like sparks.
The mounts collided, and they pressed
both head to head and chest to chest.
The shields they carried met and clashed,
the helms collided, and they crashed
together with tremendous jolts
that made a noise like thunderbolts.
When the two knights had met and striven
no rein or stirrup was unriven;
there was not one intact breast strap,
3600 and not a single girth or flap,
and even their strong saddlebows
were split and shattered by the blows,
so when the two knights fell to earth,
they were not thought of lesser worth,
since their accoutrement had failed.
They sprang right back up and assailed
each other, settling their scores
more fiercely than a pair of boars.
Without threats, they began to deal
3610 tremendous blows with swords of steel,
like those whose mutual hate is fierce.
So roughly did they tear and pierce
the helms and shining hauberk's mail,
blood sprang forth in the iron's trail.
The knights put up a splendid fight,
dealt savage blows with all their might,
and stunned each other with hard clouts.
The knights had many long, fierce bouts,
and both proved equal to the test

with neither one the worst or best.   3620
As was inevitable, the man
who crawled across the Sword-Bridge span
could feel his hands were weakening clearly,
for he had injured them severely.
The many people who were backing
this knight could see his grip was slacking;
on all sides they began to speak,
for they could see his blows grow weak,
and they were very much afraid
that he would lose and were dismayed   3630
to see the way he had the worst
of it, while Meleagant was first.
High at the tower windowsill,
a wise maid saw his loss of skill.
She pondered deep within her heart
the knight whose hands must surely smart
was hardly one to undertake
to fight this battle for her sake
or other folk of low degree.
The only way he would agree   3640
to fight it would be for the queen.
Now, if he knew she watched the scene
high at the window while he fought,
he would grow strong, the maiden thought;
the news would make him strong and bold.
The maiden gladly would have told
the knight to look around some more,
if she had known what name he bore.
She sought the queen and asked her it.
"For God's sake and your benefit,   3650
my lady, also for our own,
if you can make that knight's name known,
tell, so his name may bring him aid."
"The question you have asked me, maid,"
was the response made by the queen,
"is one in which I have not seen

a trace of treachery or spite,
but only what is good and right.
I think, if I make no mistake,

3660 his name is Lancelot of the Lake." *
"Oh, Lord! How wonderful to hear!
That fills my heart with joy and cheer!"
the maiden started to rejoice.
She leapt, and in her loudest voice
she leaned out and began to call,
so that her words were heard by all:
"Oh Lancelot! Turn round and view
the person who is watching you!"
He heard his own name; Lancelot

3670 turned quickly and looked up to spot
the very lady, as he whirled,
who was the one in all the world
that he most greatly longed to see,
high in the tower gallery.
Now that his lady had been found,
Lancelot did not turn around
or tear away his eyes or face,
but he preferred to stay in place,
defending himself from behind,

3680 which Meleagant was pleased to find.
He thought his rival undefended
and pressed him hard as they contended.
So, while the natives were elated,
the foreigners were devastated;
they could not stand up; many found
they had to lie down on the ground,
amazed and vastly ill at ease,
stretch out, or get down on their knees;
some found it joyous, some appalling.

3690 At once the maid started calling:
"Oh, Lancelot! How can it be?
How can you act so foolishly?
You once were the embodiment

of goodness and accomplishment,
the soul of prowess, good, and right.
I don't believe God made a knight
who ever could approach your claim
to valor and renown and fame;
that was the way that you once acted.
Today we see you so distracted   3700
that you strike blows behind your back   3700a
and from your rear make your attack.   3700b
To see this tower you are admiring,
the sight of it is so inspiring,
turn round and fight him from this place."
Then Lancelot felt deep disgrace;
so lowly did he rate himself
that he began to hate himself.
He had been worsted hitherto,
as every man and woman knew.
So he leapt back, turned toward the queen,
and coerced Meleagant between   3710
his body and the mighty tower.
When Meleagant used all his power
to turn back to the other side,
Lancelot rushed him as he tried
and hurled himself with so much strength,
with his whole body at full length,
and shield against the warrior,
he made him stagger twice or more
to his regret, to say the least.
His strength and boldness were increased.   3720
The help Love gave to him was great,
and he had never felt such hate
for anyone at any moment
as he felt then for his opponent.
Now Love and Hatred, great and mortal,
not seen before in any mortal,
made him so fierce and so courageous
that Meleagant found him outrageous.

Perceiving that it was no jest,
3730 he feared him and was much impressed,
for he had never known or met
so bold a knight or one who set
about him as this knight would do.
So Meleagant gladly withdrew
and dodged the blows he was assigned,
which he detested and declined.
While Lancelot voiced no threats, the power
of blows drove Meleagant toward the tower
from where the queen had come to lean.
3740 He paid much homage to the queen. . . .
He drove his foe in his assault
so close that he was forced to halt;
he would not see her anymore
if he pressed forward one step more.
So Lancelot drove Meleagant
wherever he might choose or want,
backward, forward, in between,
and made him stop before the queen,
the queen his lady, one and same,
3750 the one who set his heart aflame.
As he continued to regard her,
this burning flame increased his ardor,
so he could lead and drive his foe
wherever he would have him go!
He led him where he felt inclined;
as if one-legged, as if blind,
unwillingly his rival went.
The king could see his son too spent
to shield himself with much success.
3760 He felt compassion and distress
and would have liked to intervene.
But first he had to ask the queen
to do it in the proper way,
and so the king began to say:
"My lady, I have shown affection,

and deference, and safe protection,
since you were in my custody,
and I have done most willingly
whatever showed you reverence,
and I believe some recompense   3770
would be considered opportune.
I want to ask you for a boon
and would prefer outright rejection
unless you grant it from affection.
I can see very well my son
will lose this fight and be outdone.
I cannot say I am distressed;
the favor that I would request
is Lancelot choose not to slay
my son now he is in his sway.   3780
He wronged you both, I don't deny,
but you must not want him to die.
Your sympathy I do enlist:
tell Lancelot he must desist
and strike no more at Meleagant,
and thus, for my sake, if you want,
you can repay me for my care."
"My good sir, since it is your prayer,
I shall accord it," the queen stated.
"Though I may feel a mortal hatred   3790
for your son, whom I do despise,
you've served me well and in such wise
that, as you please, in this attack
I would have Lancelot hold back."
She said it in no undertone;
her words were overheard and known
by Lancelot and Meleagant.
A lover is obedient,
and once that he is wholly hers
he does whatever she prefers   3800
and promptly pleases his loved one,
and so should Lancelot have done,

for he loved more than Pyramus*
(could a man be more amorous?).
So Lancelot had overheard.
Once her lips formed the final word,
"Since you would have him cease to vie
and, rather, hold back, so would I,"
on no pretext would Lancelot
3810　have touched his foe or moved one jot,
not if he were to die of it.
He did not strike or move one bit,
but Meleagant struck all the same,
out of his mind with wrath and shame,
and dealt his rival many a blow,
on hearing he was brought so low
they had been forced to intervene.
The king went to the battle scene;
he came down from his tower stand
3820　to give his son a reprimand
and said immediately: "What?
Should you strike blows while he does not?
Is that a proper sort of duel?
You are so arrogant and cruel.
Now is the wrong time to be bold!
We know for certain and behold
he is the one who overcame."
But Meleagant was crazed with shame.
"You must be blind," he told the king.
3830　"I think you cannot see a thing.
A person would be blind to doubt
I had the better of our bout."
The king responded: "Oh, do tell!
These witnesses all know full well
whether you tell the truth or lies.
We know the truth and where it lies."
He told his barons they must haul
his son back now and end the brawl.
The barons hurried to obey

[106]

the king's command without delay,   3840
and Meleagant was thus retired.
But no compulsion was required
with Lancelot to pull him back.
He would have taken many a thwack
before he struck at Meleagant.
The king told his son, adamant:
"So help me Heaven, you must cease
this combat and must make a peace.
Give back the queen, do not resist.
This whole dispute must be dismissed."   3850
"What utter nonsense I have heard!
Your rambling ranting is absurd!
Just let us fight! Get out of here!
You have no right to interfere!"
The king said he would not refrain:
"for I have seen you will be slain
if I were to allow such mayhem."
"He would slay me? No, I would slay him,
I would win swiftly on my own
if you would leave us both alone   3860
and would allow us two to spar."
"God save me, how obtuse you are!
Your words won't win you anything!"
"Why not?" the son asked of the king.
"This battle will not be allowed!
I don't trust you; you are so proud
and foolish that you would be slain.
A man would have to be insane
to yearn so for his own demise,
although you do not realize.   3870
I know what hatred you must feel
because I mean to curb your zeal.
God never let me watch you slain;
the sight would cause me too much pain."
The king pursued these admonitions
till peace was granted with conditions.

The peace terms were that on the spot *
he'd give the queen to Lancelot,
if Lancelot would reappear
3880   to fight with Meleagant one year
after the challenge to the fray,
no more than one year from that day,
as Lancelot would vow and swear,
and Lancelot believed it fair.
The people all ran to the truce,
and they resolved it would produce
a battle at a court much farther;
they chose the court held by King Arthur,
the British and the Cornish lord.
3890   The queen must give them her accord,
and Lancelot must vow to grant,
if he should lose to Meleagant,
the queen would go off with the victor,
and none would stop her or restrict her.
The queen agreed she would allow it,
and Lancelot agreed to vow it.
When an agreement culminated,
they doffed their arms and separated.

THE QUEEN'S REJECTION

IN Gorre this custom was imparted:
3900   when one departed, all departed.
The prisoners escaped their lot,
and one and all blessed Lancelot,
and you may very well believe
what joy they felt at their reprieve,
and so they did, without a doubt.
The foreigners all flocked about
rejoicing greatly, filled with cheer,
and said so Lancelot could hear:

"My lord, joy set our hearts aflame
the moment that we heard your name, 3910
for we could promptly understand
that our deliverance was at hand."
This jubilation went with crushing:
the crowd was struggling and rushing
to touch their hands to Lancelot.
Those who were closest in the knot
felt far more joy than they could say.
There was both joy and wrath that day:
for those who were released from capture
abandoned themselves to their rapture; 3920
for Meleagant and for his throng
it all had gone completely wrong,
so they felt saddened and defeated.
The monarch turned back and retreated,
and he did not leave Lancelot
behind but led him from the spot.
He asked to come before the queen.
"A boon I shall not contravene,"
the king said, "for I think it fair,
and I shall show you, if you care, 3930
both her and Kay the seneschal."
Lancelot nearly took a fall,
he was so joyful and elated.
Within the hall, where the queen waited,
the king led Lancelot by the finger.
She saw the king and did not linger;
she rose to meet him and pretended
that she was terribly offended.
She stood before him with head bowed
and would not speak a word aloud. 3940
"My lady, Lancelot is here,"
the king announced the chevalier,
"he's come to see you in this room,
which pleases you, I should presume."
"To see him? I have no desire,

[109]

and no, he does not please me, sire."
"What, lady, what!" the ruler said;
he was straightforward and well bred,
"What can have put you in that mood?
3950   You show too little gratitude
toward one who served you faithfully,
his life in mortal jeopardy
at times before his journey ended,
who rescued you, and who defended
your self from Meleagant, my son,
from whom, in anger, you were won."
The queen responded with distaste:
"His time and effort were a waste,
I shan't deny it, sire, not ever.
3960   I feel no gratitude whatever."
Stunned, Lancelot tried to recover
and answered like a perfect lover:
"It hurts me, I cannot deny,
but lady, I dare not ask why."
Lancelot would have expressed
his grief; to make him more distressed,
the queen would not let him be heard,
nor would she answer him a word.
She left him stunned and filled with gloom
3970   and swept into a nearby room.
As Lancelot watched her depart,
he followed her with eyes and heart.
A little distance his eyes scanned;
the chamber was too close at hand.
They would have followed willingly
and entered too, if it could be.
The heart, which is more lord and master*
and has more power, passed in after.
The eyes remained in the arrears,
3980   out with the body, filled with tears.
In confidence, the king expounded:
"Why, Lancelot, I am dumbfounded

and wonder what it all may mean
and how it happens that the queen
would find the sight of you adverse
and would not see you or converse,
for if she ever deigned to talk,
she has no reason now to balk,
or flee your words, or to demur,
with all that you have done for her.   3990
Now tell me what grave misdemeanor
has brought about the queen's demeanor,
if you know why you were rejected."
"Sire, this was wholly unexpected.
She does not care to talk with me
or to be in my company,
which grieves me." "That is her mistake,
because you risked death for her sake,
when you embarked on this adventure.
Come, my dear friend, and let us venture   4000
to find the seneschal and chat."
"I am most eager to do that."
The pair went to the steward's bed.
The first words that the steward said
to Lancelot, once that he came,
were: "How you've covered me with shame!"
"How did I shame you, tell me what
I've done to you?" asked Lancelot.
"In what way have I hurt your pride?"
"You left me wholly mortified;   4010
you finished what I had begun
and did what I could not have done."
The king left these two knights alone
and left the chamber on his own,
and Lancelot asked Kay to state
whether his suffering was great.
"Yes," he replied, "I suffer still,★
and I have never been more ill.
I'd have died long ago, no doubt,

[111]

4020 save for the king who just went out;
in his compassion he extended
great kindness, and I was befriended.
At no time, if the king were told,
did anybody once withhold
one thing of which I was in need,
for they provided it with speed
the moment that he came to learn.
But when he did me one good turn,
then Meleagant, his wicked son,
4030 in treason not to be outdone,
would summon his physicians by
and give them orders to apply
such ointments that would kill me, rather.
I had a father and a stepfather,
for when the king had a good plaster
placed on my wounds to heal them faster
and hasten my recovery,
his own son, out of treachery,
because he wished to see me dead,
4040 would order it replaced, instead,
as hastily as he could manage,
by poisoned ointment that would damage.
I know for certain that the king
did not know what was happening.
There is no way he would abide
such felony and homicide.
Moreover, you could not have known
what nobleness the king has shown
my lady here within his power.
4050 No watch has guarded any tower
in a march, when it was of mark,
since times when Noah built the ark,
as he has guarded our own queen.
He won't allow her to be seen
even by his son, who is aggrieved
his visits only are received

before the king or multitude.
The king, we owe him gratitude,
possesses such nobility,
he's kept her in security   4060
as she arranged to be confined,
by none else were her rules designed.
The king accorded her more royal
honors knowing she was loyal.
Can what they've said to me be true:
she now feels so much wrath toward you
and finds your presence so unpleasant
that in the hearing of all present,
she would not say a single word?"
"It is the truth that you have heard,   4070
the whole truth," answered Lancelot,
"but Heavens, can you tell me what
has made the queen detest me so?"
Kay answered that he did not know.
He was astonished by the change
and thought it was extremely strange.
"Her will be done," said Lancelot,
since he could not improve his lot.
"Now I must take my leave again
and go in search of Sir Gawain.   4080
He's in this land, and we agreed
he would unswervingly proceed
to the Water Bridge that lies submerged."
From Kay's room Lancelot emerged;
he asked the king if it would suit
to grant him leave to take that route.
The ruler willingly agreed.
The prisoners whom he had freed
asked Lancelot what they should do.
He said: "Come with me, all of you   4090
who wish to come; those who prefer
the queen may stay behind with her,
not feel obliged to come with me."

All willing joined him happily,
more joyous than was customary,
while maidens who were making merry
and were caught up in their delights,
and ladies, also many knights
remained behind there with the queen.
4100   They all longed for their own demesne
and wished to travel, not to stay.
Since Sir Gawain was on his way,
the queen alone kept them detained;
within the tower she remained,
announcing that she would not stir
till news of him was brought to her.

THE QUEEN'S REPENTANCE

THROUGHOUT news was disseminated
that now the queen was liberated,
and all the prisoners were released
4110   to leave with no blame in the least
whenever they pleased or felt like leaving.
Folks asked if it was worth believing.
When people gathered, as they heard,
there was no topic they preferred,
and they were not the least annoyed
the evil bridges were destroyed.
They came and went spontaneously,
not in the way it used to be.
But when the natives were informed
4120   how finely Lancelot performed,
the people who had missed the match
went to the road they knew their catch
would travel, for the natives thought
if they could capture Lancelot
and bring him back when he was seized

[114]

the king would be extremely pleased.
Because his escort had disarmed,
they were surprised by natives, armed,
who came to capture Lancelot.
No wonder he fell to their plot,   4130
unarmed as he and his men were.
They brought him back a prisoner,
his feet tied underneath his steed.
His men protested their misdeed:
"because the king has no objection;
we all enjoy the king's protection
and have safe-conduct when we travel."
They answered, "That we can't unravel,
but as our captives we'll transport
your escort and you back to court."   4140
The news about his men took wing,
until the rumor reached the king
that Lancelot was slain when caught.
The king was terribly distraught
and swore by far more than his head
that he would see the killers dead:
if the assassins could be found,
he'd have them hanged or burned or drowned.
There was no way to justify it,
if they attempted to deny it   4150
he'd disbelieve them from the start.
They'd put such wrath within his heart
and caused him to feel so ashamed
that he would be reproached and blamed
if this misdeed were not avenged;
have no doubt he would be revenged.
This rumor spread to every scene.*
It was recounted to the queen
at table, when she had been seated.
Once she had heard the lies repeated   4160
and had believed them true herself,
the shocked queen nearly slew herself

and felt so shattered and so bleak
she found she almost could not speak.
At last, quite openly she spoke
and said before the waiting folk,
"His death has left me deeply grieved.
I am not wrong to feel bereaved;
for my sake to this land he came,
4170   so I may mourn him without blame."
So she would not be overheard,
in a low murmur she averred,
that no one ever was to think
of asking her to eat or drink,
if it were true, as they had said,
the man for whom she lived was dead.
Grief-stricken, she arose and went.
She left the table to lament
where none could overhear her cries.
4180   She was so bent on her demise
that she kept clutching at her throat
as she accused herself, and smote
herself in guilt, and beat her breast.
In solitude the queen confessed
the sinfulness that she had shown
toward Lancelot, whom she had known
had always been hers, of free will,
and, had he lived, would be hers still.
For cruelty the queen upbraided
4190   herself until her beauty faded.
Her cruelty and her betrayal
made her turn withered, drawn, and pale,
as did her wakefulness and fast.
She brooded over her amassed
misdeeds, remembered and reviewed them,
and summed them up, and deeply rued them.
"Alas! What was I thinking of?★
Before me came the one I love;
I did not deign to speak a greeting

[116]

or even hear him at our meeting!   4200
When I withheld my glance, my word,*
was not what I had done absurd?
Absurd, God; was I not a fool?
Yes, I betrayed him; I was cruel.
I did it only as a jest,
but all the same he never guessed.
His pardon I shall never know,
and no one dealt the mortal blow
except myself or hurt him sorely.
When smilingly he came before me   4210
believing that I would rejoice
and see him very much by choice,
and I would not give him one look,
was that a mortal blow he took?
No conversation would I start;
I'm certain I tore out his heart
and life together; I suppose
that he was slain by those two blows,
by those Brabanters,* those alone.
Oh Heaven! How can I atone   4220
for such a murder, such a sin?
The sea, before I can begin,
and streams will all evaporate.
Alas! The comfort would be great,
and I would feel much more resigned
about his death had I entwined
my love in my arms once before.
So I could have enjoyed him more,
I wish we had been skin to skin.
Now he is dead and I would sin   4230
if I preferred to stay alive.
Once he is dead, if I survive,
would not my life be misery,
when nothing in it pleases me
except this suffering I bear?
Once he is dead, it's only fair

to suffer as I now entreat,
in life he would have found it sweet.
Vile she who would prefer to end

4240   her life than suffer for her friend,
and I am finding it a pleasure
to mourn him lengthily at leisure.
Better to live and suffer blows
than die and be in sweet repose."
The queen refused to eat or drink.
Two days of mourning* made them think
her grief and fast had left her dead.
By many are false rumors spread,
and ugly ones, not fair, they choose.

4250   Thus Lancelot received the news
his lady and his love had died.
He was appalled and horrified,
for none would think it curious
that he was grieved and furious.
His sorrow left him sorely wracked;
if you would learn what is but fact,
he held his life in such disdain
by his own hand he would be slain,
but first he voiced the grief he felt.

4260   From round his waist he took his belt,
formed one end in a sliding noose,
and told himself, his tears profuse:
"Ah, Death, you've followed me with stealth
and struck me down in perfect health!
I feel no pain in any part
except the sorrow in my heart.
That grief is painful, even killing.
I want it fatal and, God willing,
the pain will lead to my demise.

4270   What? Can I not die otherwise,
if God should prove to be unwilling?
I shall, if He permits my pulling
this belt loop tight around my throat,

[118]

so I can force Death to garrote
and murder me against her will.
This Death, who only seeks to kill
those who avoid her, has not felt
inclined to come here, yet my belt
will make of Death a captive whole.
Once she is under my control,   4280
she will do as I think becoming.
True, she will be too slow in coming;
my yearning for her is the stronger."
Then Lancelot delayed no longer.
Over his head he pulled the noose
down to his neck to be of use
to choke himself, and then he bound
the other end of his belt round
the pommel of his saddle bow,
so furtively that none would know,   4290
then let himself slip to the ground
to have his horse drag him around
till he expired. He set no store
on lingering on one hour more.
When those who rode with Lancelot
saw he had fallen at that spot,
they thought it was a fainting spell,
because the riders could not tell
around his neck a noose was laced.
The riders picked him up in haste;   4300
within their arms they held him fast
and found the noose that he had passed
around his neck destructively,
to make him his worst enemy.
Immediately they cut the noose.
His throat had suffered such abuse,
some time elapsed before he spoke,
because he very nearly broke
the veins within his neck and throat,
so punishing was his garrote.   4310

[119]

Had he desired, he could not manage
to do himself more harm or damage.
He burned with grief and thought it hard
that they had placed him under guard;
if no constraints had been applied,
he'd have committed suicide.
When he could harm himself no more,
he shouted, "Ha! Death, you vile whore,
by God, why didn't you possess
4320   the power and courageousness
to kill me in place of my lady?
Afraid to do a good deed, maybe;
you would not deign to do my will.
Death, you are reprehensible
and always will be counted such.
Oh! What a kindness! It's too much!
Aren't you so favorably inclined
toward me! Curse him who thinks you kind
or who feels grateful on that score!
4330   I do not know who hates me more:
Life, who desires me and would stay me,
or Death, who does not wish to slay me,
and thus one and the other kill.
I ought to live against my will;
So help me Heaven, it is right.
I should have killed myself outright
the moment that my lady queen
had shown me such a hateful mien.
Her act was not unmotivated:
4340   there was good reason why she hated,
but I do not know what it was.
If only I had known the cause
before her soul reached Heaven's throne,
I would have managed to atone
as she desired in any fashion,
so she'd have shown me her compassion.
Oh, God, what could have been my crime?

I think she learned about the time
I mounted in the cart that shamed me.
I don't know why she would have blamed me   4350
except the cart. That was ill-fated.
But if the cart had made me hated,
my God, why was this crime my doom?
For anyone who would presume
to chide me never knew Love well,
because no one could ever tell
a deed performed at Love's behooving
would be considered worth reproving.
It's love and courtesy when done
to honor the beloved one.   4360
I did not do it for my love.
Alas! What am I speaking of?
What lover ought I to proclaim?
I dare not give the queen this name.
But Love has left me well apprised:
I ought not to have been despised;
if she had loved me, I contend
she should have called me her true friend,
for I felt honored and required
to do whatever Love desired,   4370
down to the cart: I mounted it.
As Love she should have counted it,
because Love truly was its source.
Love tests her own thus, in due course,
and knows her own by such a measure.
And yet my lady took no pleasure
in services that she received,
as, when I found her, I perceived
most clearly by her mien and face,
although her lover chose disgrace   4380
and often was reproached and shamed.
I did this deed, and I am blamed.
I found it sweet, and now it's bitter.
My word, her actions would be fitter

for persons who know nothing of
what it is like to be in love,
immersing honor in disgrace;*
it is not cleansed but soiled and base.
So persons who do not discover
4390   Love cheerfully despise a lover.
They do not fear commands of Love,
of whom they think themselves above,
while those who do as Love behooved
find they are always much improved,
and everything is pardonable;
he errs who fails to do Love's will."
So Lancelot mourned and complained.
His people, holding him restrained,
lamented with him, mourned and grieved.
4400   By then more news had been received:
the queen was actually not dead.
Then Lancelot was comforted.
If formerly he spent his breath
on loud laments about her death,
the joy he felt when he was told
increased a hundred thousandfold.
From six or seven leagues away
from where King Bademagu held sway
(they were no further from that spot)
4410   the good news came of Lancelot.
King Bademagu most gladly found
he came back living, hale, and sound.
Well-mannered and of courtly mien,
he went to notify the queen.
She answered, "Good sir, since you said it,
in turn I give your statement credit,
and I shall take you at your word,
but if he had died, rest assured
I would eternally have banished
4420   good cheer; my joy would all have vanished;
if some knight in my service had

met death, I would be very sad."
The king departed from the queen,
who waited, far less than serene,
to meet her lover and her joy.
She sought no longer to annoy
or be severe with him at all.
Meanwhile the rumors did not pall
but kept on spreading undeterred,
until the queen quite promptly heard   4430
that Lancelot had meant to die
for her if they had let him try.
She was delighted by the news,
but for no reason would she choose
to have misfortune be his lot.
Within the meantime, Lancelot
arrived in a tremendous haste.
The king ran up, and they embraced
the moment that he came in sight.
His joyfulness made him so light,   4440
he thought he might have sprouted wings.
And yet the great joy of the king's
was promptly curtailed when he found
those who held Lancelot fast bound.
The king told them their fate was dread,
and they were all disgraced and dead.
Immediately they told their sire
they thought the capture his desire.
"How could you think of such a thing?
You did not shame him," said the king.   4450
"The shame is mine and the objection;
he traveled under my protection,
so you will find it is no jape,
if you endeavor to escape."
When Lancelot heard how he fumed,
his energies were all consumed
by peacemaking, however stressful,
until his efforts were successful.

The king took him to see the queen.
4460 Most certainly she did not mean
to meet her knight with eyes cast down.
She showed she thought him of renown
and happily went up to meet him,
deciding at her side to seat him.
Then he and she conversed at leisure
of anything that gave them pleasure,
and they did not lack subject matter:
Love furnished them much of the latter.
When he could see the time was right,
4470 his words all caused the queen delight,
then Lancelot chose to confide:
"My lady, I am mystified
you would have acted in that way
the day before the previous day,
when you would not speak one word to me.
My lady queen, you nearly slew me.
I did not have the fortitude,
as I do now, to dare allude
to it and ask you the offense.
4480 Now I shall offer recompense,
but tell me how I have transgressed,
because I am so much distressed."
Then in her turn the queen exclaimed:
"What was it? Were you not ashamed *
about the cart and much afraid?
The two full paces you delayed
before you climbed into the cart
showed great reluctance on your part,
and it was for this reason, true,
4490 I would not speak or look at you."
Said Lancelot: "Another time
God safeguard me from such a crime.
May Heaven's mercy be denied
if you were not well justified.
My lady, grant me your permission

[124]

to make amends and have remission;
for God's sake say you will agree."
"I pardon you most willingly.
Friend, you are totally excused
for that of which you are accused."   4500
"Lady," he said, "I thank you well,
but in here I can hardly tell
the things to you that give me pleasure.
I would converse at greater leisure,
if such talk might be contemplated."
In answer the queen indicated
a window, but with eyes, not finger.
She said: "Come talk with me and linger
beside this window in the night,
when everyone is sleeping tight;   4510
into that orchard you must venture.
Of course your body cannot enter
this chamber, nor can it abide.
I shall be in and you outside,
for you cannot come in with me,
nor can I reach you physically
save with my words or with my hand.
But, if you please, there I shall stand
for love of you till day is near.
We cannot be together here,*   4520
for in my chamber opposite
lies Kay the Seneschal, unfit,
covered with wounds, and weak and sore.
You would not find an open door,
but firmly closed and well protected.
Take care you come here undetected,
so that no spy finds you nearby."
"I shan't be seen by any spy
to think ill or speak ill of it,
my lady, if I can permit."   4530
The tryst arranged, they separated,
and so they parted, much elated.

OUT of the room went Lancelot,
so very happy he could not
recall one hardship or one woe.
In coming nightfall was too slow,
and longer was the day persisting,
for all the trials he'd been resisting,
than a hundred days or one whole year.
4540   For he would eagerly appear
to talk, if night would but descend.
At last the day drew to an end;
by pitch-black night it was beset.
Night tucked day in its coverlet *
and wrapped it in its cloak overlaid.
When Lancelot saw daylight fade,
he feigned he was not feeling strong
and claimed he'd been awake too long
and must rest, being tired and lame.
4550   Those of you who have done the same
will know why he feigned being tired
to those who lodged him and retired.
His bed was of no interest,
and nothing could have made him rest,
because he could not and dared not;
no interest had Lancelot
in power and boldness for repose.
Soon, quietly, the knight arose,
and he would not be found maligning
4560   that no moon and no stars were shining,
or, in the house, no candlestick
or lantern with a burning wick,
or lighted lamp was to be found.
He went out looking all around,
lest someone see him as he went,
for everyone believed he spent

the night in bed, by sleep transported.
Without companions, unescorted,
he went directly and alone
to where the orchard trees were grown,   4570
and as good fortune should befall,
a portion of the orchard wall
had fallen in the recent past,
so through this gap he swiftly passed
and came before the window sill,
and there he stood so very still
that he did not once cough or sneeze.
Attired in a pure white chemise,
the queen appeared. She wore no coat
or tunic with her petticoat,   4580
but a short mantle covered her
of scarlet cloth and marmot fur.
When Lancelot beheld the queen
and window where she came to lean,
its heavy bars a barrier,
with gentleness he greeted her,
and equal tenderness inspired her,
for Lancelot greatly desired her,
and she was in the selfsame mood.   *Consent*
On nothing that was dull or crude   4590
did they take counsel or expand;
instead they held each other's hand.
Ever more closely they were drawn
to one another, woebegone
that they could not be closer still,
so they bemoaned the iron grill.
Lancelot boasted with some pride,
if the queen wanted him inside,
she should not have the slightest doubt:
no iron bars could keep him out.   4600
She said: "These bars, make no mistake,
are stiff to bend and tough to break!
There is no way that you could twist

[127]

or pull one toward you with your fist,
or tear these bars out of their bed."
"Don't be concerned," he promptly said.
"My lady, to be where you are,
I would not heed an iron bar.
All that can keep me out is you;
4610   no entry then would I pursue.
If you allow me to come near,
the way to you is wholly clear,
and yet, if you do not consent,
that is such an impediment,
there is no way I would proceed."
She said: "I wish you would indeed;
my wishes are no obstacle.
But you must wait a bit until
I reach my bed, where I am bound,
4620   and then you must not make a sound,
for it would be no joke or jest
to wake the seneschal at rest
by any noise that we might cause.
I think I ought to go, because
he would not be too understanding
if he should see me where I'm standing."
"Then, lady, go away from here,"
said Lancelot, "but have no fear
that any noisiness will jar.
4630   I think I can slip out each bar
so that no effort need be taken
and nobody within will waken."
The queen turned from him to depart,
and Lancelot prepared to start
to free the window that was barred.
He seized, and pulled, and tugged so hard
upon the bars set in their base,
he bent and pulled them out of place.
The iron was so sharp to bend,
4640   he cut his little finger's end

down to the nerve at that one point,
and afterward the whole first joint
of his next fingertip was gashed.
He did not notice he was slashed
or blood was dripping with his pulse.
He was intent on something else.
The window sill was far from low,
yet Lancelot swung from below
and quickly slipped into the keep.
He found Kay in his bed asleep,   4650
and then he went to the queen's bed,
and worshipped her, and bowed his head;
no relic left him so devout.
To him in turn the queen held out
her arms, embraced her knight, and pressed
and held him closely to her breast.
She drew him down into her bed
beside her and exhibited
as much warmth as she could impart,
inspired by love and by her heart.   4660
Love made her greet him with delight;
if she felt great love for her knight,
he felt a hundred thousand more.
Never had any heart such store
of love as his. When Love arrived,
all other hearts were much deprived,
for Love soon entered in his heart,
pervading it in every part.
Then Lancelot had what he sought,
when the queen showed how much she thought   4670
of his companionship and charms,
when he could hold her in his arms,
and she could hold him in her own.
So tender was her love-play shown,
her touch, the kisses she dispensed,
that truly they experienced
a joy and wonder that occurred,

the like of which was never heard.
I shall be still about their rapture,
4680   one which an author should not capture
in tales that are respectable.
Of joys the most delectable,
supreme of joys that one can feel
is one the story shall conceal,
but Lancelot, throughout that night,
felt greatest joy and sheer delight.
He had to rise, upon the morrow,
from his love's side, much to his sorrow.
He rose from the queen's bed a martyr,
4690   he was so tortured a departer.
His suffering became so keen,
his heart went over to the queen,
and Lancelot was forced to leave it;
he lacked the power to retrieve it.
It found the queen so very thrilling,
it would abandon her unwilling.
The body left, the heart stayed still.
He went straight toward the window sill.
Enough of his shed blood remained
4700   to spot the sheets and leave them stained,
for from his fingers blood had flowed.
Lancelot left the queen's abode
repressing tears and full of sighs,
and he could only agonize.
They'd set no other rendezvous,
which grieved him, but it would not do.
He crossed the window sill downcast,
where he so eagerly had passed.
His fingers had been badly mangled.
4710   He straightened out the bars he'd tangled,
and he replaced them in their track.
From side to side or front to back
the iron bars revealed no trace
they had been bent or pulled from place.

[130]

He acted toward the room he'd known
as if it were an altarstone:
he turned to it, and genuflected,
and left it utterly dejected.
He met no man who knew his face
until he reached his lodging place.   4720
Upon his bed he lay down nude,
as if he'd slept in solitude
and woke nobody from his rest.
At prime, though he was not distressed,
with great surprise he contemplated
his fingers, which were lacerated.
Since he was certain on this score:
he hurt himself because he tore
the iron bars out of the wall,
he did not feel annoyed at all.   4730
He'd have preferred to let somebody
pull both his arms out of his body
than fail to pass within the shut
bedchamber, elsewise, had he cut
his fingers with two wounds that bad,
he would have been annoyed and sad.

LEGAL COMBAT

THE morning found the queen asleep,*
and she was lying lost in deep,
sound slumber in her curtained room.
She certainly did not presume   4740
her sheets were bloodstained; no, the queen
believed them seemly and pristine.
As soon as Meleagant was dressed
and outfitted, the knight progressed
toward the room she was occupying
and entered where the queen was lying.

He found she had begun to stir
and noticed her white bedsheets were
smeared with fresh bloodstains and bespotted.
4750   He showed his comrades what he'd spotted
and nudged them. With an evil mind
he looked at Kay's bed, quick to find
his sheets had bloodstains on the white;
his wounds had opened in the night.
"Well, lady," thundered Meleagant,
"now I have found the signs I want.
He is a fool who labors hard*
to keep a woman under guard
in an attempt to keep her chaste.
4760   His pains and effort are a waste.
Who guards her close will lose her faster
4762   than one unheeding of disaster.
4762a   My father was a splendid guard,
4762b   protecting you from me so hard!
From me he guarded you all right,
but Kay the seneschal, last night,
despite all that the king could do,
looked on and had his will of you,
and I can prove it very well."
"How?" asked the queen. "Since I must tell,
I've found as proof of your offense
4770   blood on your sheets for evidence.
That is my proof; I've understood;
Kay's wounds are open, and the blood
is on his sheets and on your own.
The proof of it is clearly shown."
That was the first time that the queen
observed, amazed by what she'd seen,
the bloody sheets upon each bed.
She was ashamed and blushed bright red.
"God save me," she began to say,
4780   "this blood has never come from Kay
that I see stained my sheets of white.

[132]

I had a nosebleed in the night;
I think it must be from my nose."
And so she truly did suppose.
"By my head," answered Meleagant,
"your protest is irrelevant.
We don't need any lies from you
with your misconduct proven true.
It is a simple thing to prove."
Then he said, "Gentlemen, don't move,"   4790
(to the guards who were standing there)
"till I return, and take good care
the bedsheets are not taken hence.
When he has seen the evidence,
I want the king to think me sound."
Meleagant searched until he found
the king and fell down at his feet.
"Sire, come and see, I do entreat,
what you could never have foreseen.
Do come along and see the queen.   4800
You will see wonders verified
I have discovered and espied.
I pray that justice will prevail,
and promise me you will not fail
to honor and uphold my rights,
before you go to see these sights.
You know I put myself at stake
in this adventure for her sake,
and now you are my enemy,
for you protect the queen from me.   4810
Her bed shows, in this morning's light,
that Kay has lain with her each night;
I saw it clearly as I gazed.
By God, sire, do not be amazed
if I complain and find it painful
that toward me she would be disdainful.
That she would hate me I despise,
while every night with Kay she lies."

The king said, "Hush! That sounds absurd."
4820 "Then if you will not take my word,
see the condition of her sheets
the way Kay left them with his feats.
You think I lie but will discover
that I can show you sheets and cover
besmirched with blood and badly stained
by injuries that Kay sustained."
"Come," said the king, "and I shall view.
My eyes will tell me what is true."
Immediately he went around
4830 to seek the bedroom, where he found
the queen arising from her bed.
He saw the sheets, bloodstained and red,
and Kay's bed looking just the same.
"My lady, this is cause for shame,
and you and Kay would be undone,
if truth were spoken by my son."
"So help me God," was her reply.
"No one has told so foul a lie,
not even in the worst of dreams.
4840 To me the seneschal Kay seems
so loyal, courteous, and just,
no deed of his inspires distrust.
As for my body, I declare
I do not sell it in the fair
or peddle or give it away.
Such outrage would not come from Kay,
nor would I be the least inclined."
Said Meleagant, "Sire, be so kind
as to arrange for Kay to pay
4850 for such an outrage in a way
that puts the queen in deep disgrace.
As fount of justice in this place,
I ask you and beseech you, father.
Kay has betrayed his lord King Arthur,
whose trust in him was shown so sweeping

[134]

that he once placed in Kay's safe-keeping
the one whom he most loved on earth."
"Sire, let me answer to his worth;
I will acquit myself," Kay hurled.
"When I leave for a better world,   4860
God have no mercy on my soul
if by my lady on one sole
occasion did I ever lie.
This day I would prefer to die
than have committed so abhorred
and foul a crime against my lord.
God never grant me better health,
but kill me now, if I'd the stealth
even to have considered it.
Last night the blood my wounds emit   4870
flowed in a hemorrhage, unrestrained,
and that is how my sheets were stained.
Your son may view me with mistrust,
but he is certainly unjust."
Said Meleagant: "God grant me aid,
some wicked fiends left you betrayed,
because last night excessive ardor
made you exert yourself the harder,
until your wounds were open wide.
No use, it cannot be denied.   4880
The evidence of what I've said
is stains of blood upon each bed,
which are apparent at this time.
Men should be made to pay for crime,
when it is proved and they are caught.
Never has a warrior sought
such scandal when he'd earned your fame,
and so you have been brought to shame."
"Sire, sire," Kay promised to the king,
"whatever charge your son may bring,   4890
I shall disprove his accusations
and shall defend our reputations.

I have endured such torment rarely,
for he belabors me unfairly."
The king said: "You should not exert
in battle; you are badly hurt."
"My lord, if only you permit,
ill as I am and as unfit,
I mean to fight with him to show

4900   his accusation false and low.
I am completely innocent."
The queen in secrecy had sent
to Lancelot, and she contended
the seneschal would be defended
before the ruler by a knight,
if Meleagant would dare to fight.
"You could not find," was his reply,
"a knight with whom I would not vie
in combat on the battlefield

4910   till one of us was forced to yield,
unless the warrior were a giant."
Then Lancelot arrived, compliant.
The room was crammed and put to strain
by knights who crowded in his train.
Then all, young and gray-headed, heard
the queen relate what had occurred.
She told him promptly when he came,
"Lancelot, I am put to shame.
What Meleagant has just confected

4920   will mean that I shall be suspected
by all who heeded Meleagant,
if you do not make him recant.
Because my sheets and those of Kay
are bloodstained, he has tried to say
Kay lay with me and has predicted
that Kay will surely be convicted,
if he cannot beat Meleagant,
or if another does not want
to help by being substituted,

[136]

so that the charge can be refuted." 4930
"While you have me about the place,
you never need to plead your case,
and God forbid," said Lancelot,
"that such of you or him be thought,
or that you merit such suspicion.
I'm set to fight and in condition;
if I have any strength in me,
I'll use all my ability
defending Kay from what was said
and shall do battle in his stead." 4940
Then Meleagant leapt up and swore:
"God save me, that would please me more,
let no one think that it would not."
"Sir king," continued Lancelot,*
"I know of trials, suits, verdicts, laws;
a battle for so grave a cause
requires an oath from either side."
With promptness Meleagant replied,
because he was in no way torn:
"Indeed, then let the oath be sworn. 4950
Bring out the relics straightaway;
I know I've rightfully blamed Kay."
That Lancelot chose to deny:
"For Kay was never known to lie
in such a case, God grant me aid."
They shouted for their arms and made
the people tending to their needs
go out of doors and fetch their steeds.
The horses were delivered armed.
The squires armed them, and they were armed. 4960
The relics were brought and kept out.
Upon which Meleagant stepped out,
and at his side was Lancelot.
They knelt together on the spot,
and Meleagant, while speaking loud,
stretched out his hand to them and vowed:

"So help me God and His saints all,
I swear that Kay the seneschal
was sharing the queen's bed at night
4970 and with her found complete delight."
"I swear you are a perjurer;
I swear Kay never lay with her
or touched her," Lancelot replied.
"If Heaven please, on him who lied
God's vengeance fall unmitigated,
and let the truth be demonstrated.
But I shall take another vow
and swear an oath before you now,
no matter who may be distressed,
4980 if it turns out I get the best
of Meleagant, let it be known,
so help me God and God alone
and relics: in this controversy
I'll never show him any mercy."
When he had heard this oath employed,
the king was far from overjoyed.
After each knight had taken oath,
the horses were brought out for both,
in all ways they were fine indeed.
4990 Then each knight mounted his good steed,
and each one rode against his foe
as swiftly as a horse could go,
and at their horses' fastest gait
they struck each other blows so great,
of the two lances they had clasped,
the hafts were all their fists had grasped.
Upon the ground both lay outspread,
but they were not ones to play dead;
each knight leapt up immediately
5000 and strove to cause an injury,
so naked swords could leave their marks.
Blows to their helmets cast off sparks
that flew straight up into the sky.

So wrathfully did both knights vie,
using the naked swords they held,
that as their sword blades were propelled
backward and forth, they traded blows
and would not seek enough repose
to have time to regain their wind.
The king was terribly chagrined, 5010
and so he called upon the queen,
who had gone up the stair to lean
over the tower's high arcade.
"By the Creator," the king prayed,
"allow the two to separate."
"Exactly as you indicate,"
the queen responded loyally,
"You will not be opposed by me."
Now Lancelot had clearly heard
the king and what he had preferred 5020
and what the queen said in replying.
Immediately he stopped his vying,
for he was disinclined to duel,
while Meleagant kept striking, cruel,
and did not wish to take repose.
The king came in between the foes
and held his son, while his son swore,
"I do not wish for peace, but war."
He had no interest in a peace.
The king said: "Let your talking cease, 5030
believe me, you will show discretion.
You may be sure my intercession
will cause no shame or harm to you;
do what you are required to do.
How could your memory be so short?
Have you not pledged, at Arthur's court,
to battle there with Lancelot?
You ought to realize, do you not,
the honor will be greater there,
if it is yours, than anywhere?" . 5040

[139]

These were the arguments he made
to try to make his son be staid,
till he calmed him and got them parted.

LANCELOT'S BETRAYAL

THEN Lancelot, keen to get started
and find where Sir Gawain had been,
came to the king and then the queen
and sought permission to depart.
With their leave he rode out to start
toward the Water Bridge. The entourage
5050 of knights escorting him was large,
but many who were in his train
were wishing that they could remain.
They made good use of every day
until they were one league away
and had come in the vicinage
of the Underwater Bridge.
Before they saw its workmanship,
a little dwarf who held a whip
to threaten and chastise his mount,
5060 so he could call him to account,
came up to meet them on the road
on the large hunter that he rode.
Immediately the dwarf demanded,
the way that he had been commanded:
"Which one of you is Lancelot?
I am on your side, so do not
conceal it, tell the truth of it;
I ask it for your benefit."
So Lancelot owned to his name.
5070 "I am that man, the very same
for whom you search," he said forthright.
"Oh, Lancelot, my noble knight,

leave all these people on their own;
trust me, and come with me alone.
The place I'll lead you is a prize.
Let no one follow with his eyes.
Let them await you on this track,
for in no time we shall be back."
Since no suspicions crossed his mind,
he had his people stay behind   5080
and sought the dwarf out, who betrayed him.
The people who had come to aid him
could wait at length for Lancelot;
once he fell victim to their plot
his captors had no wish to yield him.
When passing time had not revealed him,
lamenting started to ensue.
His people wondered what to do.
They said the dwarf must have deceived
their Lancelot and loudly grieved,   5090
it would be foolishness to doubt.
They sadly tried to seek him out
but knew not where he might be found
nor to what parts he might be bound.
They all thought counsel indispensable.
Those who were wisest and most sensible
took counsel and, I think, agreed
first to the Bridge they would proceed,
the passage being near the spot,
and after search for Lancelot   5100
with the advice of Sir Gawain,
if they found him in wood or plain.
With this good counsel all concurred
so heartily that none demurred.
To the Water Bridge went every man;
as soon as they had reached its span
they saw the lord Gawain full well.
He teetered on the bridge and fell
into the water, deep and dank.

[141]

5110   Sometimes he rose and sometimes sank;
now he appeared; now he was lost.
With branches, poles, and sticks they crossed
the gulf and reached to pull him back.
He'd but his hauberk on his back;
upon his head his helm was pressed;
it was worth ten of all the rest;
his cuisses rusted up with sweat,
because Gawain had been beset
and suffered hardship, many dangers,
5120   and overcome assaults from strangers.
The horse and lance and shield he bore
were over on the other shore.
They pulled him from the stream alive
and did not think he would survive;
so waterlogged was Sir Gawain,
until he coughed it up again
he was not fit to say one word.
When finally he could be heard,
and voice and chest and throat were clear,
5130   his voice regained so they could hear,
as soon as Sir Gawain could speak
and found his tone of voice less weak,
he asked the people on the scene
to give him tidings of the queen,
if they could tell him any news.
They answered that she did not choose
to part from King Bademagu,
for he did all that he could do
to honor her and serve her well.
5140   The lord Gawain asked them to tell:
"Did anyone go in that banned
country to seek her in that land?"
They answered: "Yes, make no mistake,
the man was Lancelot of the Lake
who crossed the Sword Bridge span, and sought
and freed the queen, and when he fought

he freed us too and came to aid us.
But afterward a dwarf betrayed us.
A smirking little dwarf with thick
humpback has played a filthy trick   5150
and taken Lancelot from us
to someplace most mysterious."
The lord asked: "When did this occur?"
"The dwarf took him today, good sir,
nearby here, as our retinue
and he approached in search of you."
"And how has Lancelot acquitted
himself here once he was admitted?"
The escort started to recount
a detailed, blow-by-blow account,   5160
not leaving out a single word,
and told Gawain the queen preferred
to wait for him, and do believe
she could not be induced to leave
until she saw him once again,
since she had news of Sir Gawain.
The lord asked how they were inclined:
"When we have left this bridge behind,
shall we go seeking Lancelot?"
It would be best, the party thought,   5170
if they returned to find the queen
and let the monarch intervene,
lest Meleagant, whose hate ran deep,
had treacherously placed him in keep.
If the king knew wherever his son
had Lancelot or what he'd done,
he would ensure he was returned,
so they could wait until they learned.
All thought this counsel should be heeded,
and back to court they all proceeded.   5180
The king and queen were waiting there.
Together with the regal pair
awaited Kay, the steward royal,

[143]

and, filled with treason and disloyal,
the traitor who had caused them great
concern for Lancelot and his fate
and filled all those who came with dread.
They thought he was betrayed and dead
and loudly mourned, for they were grieved.
5190 The sorry news that she received
distressed the queen and made her grave,
but she endeavored to behave
with all the graciousness she might.
She was supposed to feel delight
at Sir Gawain, which she did feel,
and yet the queen did not conceal
the grief she could not help but show.
She had to show both joy and woe:
for Lancelot her heart did ache;
5200 for Sir Gawain and for his sake
she made it seem that she rejoiced.
But all to whom the news was voiced
were deeply saddened, and they anguished
to learn that Lancelot had vanished.
The king would not have had to feign
his joy at meeting Sir Gawain,
which would have brought him joyfulness,
but felt such sorrow and distress
for Lancelot, lost and deceived,
5210 that he was both amazed and grieved.
The queen insisted, without fail,
the king must search up hill, down dale,
throughout his land without delay,
as did the lord Gawain and Kay.
Each person at the ruler's court
began to urge him and exhort:
the search must start immediately.
"Now just leave the affair to me,"
the king replied, "and say no more,
5220 for I was ready long before

and need no prayer or request
to send my searchers on their quest."
Before him every knee was bent.
The king immediately sent
his messengers: armed men, well known,
whose great discretion had been shown,
who went throughout his kingdom's span
for news about the missing man.
They asked all over of his fate
and yet heard nothing accurate.   5230
They had no news when they returned
to where the warriors sojourned.
Gawain, and Kay, and all the rest
said they would search, with lance at rest,
completely armed and helmeted,
and would send no one in their stead.
One day past dinner, when they all
were being armed within the hall,
since it was time for them to ride,
a youth appeared, and came inside,   5240
and walked amid them and between
until he came before the queen.
She was not rosy of complexion,
for she had felt such deep dejection
and had so mourned for Lancelot,
of whom no tidings had been brought,
her coloring had greatly paled.
She was the one the youth first hailed,
and then, nearby her, he addressed
the king and turned to greet the rest,   5250
including Sir Gawain and Kay.
He had a letter to convey
to the king, which he promptly handed.
The ruler openly commanded
the letter read within their hearing.
The reader knew what was appearing
upon the parchment and repeated

that Lancelot, in writing, greeted
the king, his good lord, and commended
5260   the services he had extended,
and thanked him for all he had done
to do him honor there, as one
in every way at his command.
They all should clearly understand
he was with Arthur, fit and strong,
and asked the queen to come along;
he ordered her upon her way,
and with her Sir Gawain and Kay.
The letter, as the reader read it,
5270   had seals enough to give it credit.
It looked authentic, they believed,
and they were joyous and relieved.
The court resounded with delight;
the following day, when it was light,
they said they would be on their way.
Next morning, at the break of day
they dressed, sought armor, gear, and tack,
arose, and mounted, and rode back.
The king accompanied them some measure
5280   with greatest joy and greatest pleasure,
and rode a long way with their band,
escorting them out of his land.
Then he took leave, across the border,
first of the queen, as was in order,
and then of all the rest combined.
The queen showed great presence of mind
and gratefully chose to refer
to all that he had done for her.
Arms round his neck, the queen's proposal
5290   was to be at the king's disposal
for services she could accord,
as would her husband and her lord.
There was no more she could extend.
Then Sir Gawain, as lord and friend,

made him this promise, as did Kay.
Then they proceeded on their way.
To Heaven's care the king addressed
these three, before he hailed the rest
and after started to return.
The queen did not choose to sojourn 5300
a single day throughout that week,
and neither did her escort seek
repose until the news was broached
at court that Arthur's queen approached.
When news so joyful was imparted,
King Arthur felt glad and lighthearted
about his nephew, when he learned.
He thought the queen had been returned
with Kay and other lesser folk
by his bold deeds and master stroke. 5310
It was not as he postulated.
The town was utterly vacated,
for everyone went out to meet them,
and all they met began to greet them,
whether of knightly class or mean:
"Hail Sir Gawain, who brought the queen,
and many ladies in deplored
and captive state, and who restored
so many of our prisoners."
To them Gawain responded: "Sirs, 5320
your praise of me is without merit;
I don't deserve a bit of credit.
Immediately cease to acclaim me,
because these honors only shame me.
I did not come in time that day
and failed because of my delay,
but Lancelot arrived in time,
and he won honors so sublime,
no knight has been so eminent."
"Dear sir, please tell us where he went; 5330
we do not see him in your train."

"Where is he?" answered Sir Gawain.
"At my lord king's court, is he not?"
"My word, there is no Lancelot
at court or elsewhere in this land.
No news of him has come to hand,
not since my ladyship's abduction."
By Sir Gawain's abrupt deduction,
the letter that they had received
5340   was forged, and they had been deceived.
The letter had been their betrayal.
Then there resounded cry and wail.
Lamenting they returned to court.
King Arthur asked them to report
immediately about the case,
and there were many in that place
to tell how Lancelot behaved,
how through great efforts he had saved
the queen and set the captives free,
5350   and how and by what treachery
the dwarf had taken him from them.
The king found much there to condemn
and was downcast and deeply grieved,
and yet his heart was so relieved
by his great joy about the queen
that joyfulness did contravene
grief till, with her whom he loved best,
he'd scant concern about the rest.

THE TOURNAMENT

WHILE she was outside the dominion
5360   if I may give you my opinion,
the maids and ladies in its bourn
who were unmarried and forlorn
convened and thought it opportune

[148]

for them to marry very soon.
They settled at this parliament
upon a splendid tournament,
which to this end they would employ.
The Lady of Pomelegoi
was challenged by the Lady of Worstede.*
To fighters who were badly worsted 5370
the ladies would have nought to tell,
but to those fighters who did well
they'd say their love might well be claimed.
The tournament would be proclaimed
in lands afar and proximate,
and they would have the tourney date
announced long prior to the event,
so that more people would be sent.
The queen returned home from her journey
within this time before the tourney. 5380
The moment that they came to learn
about the queen and her return,
the ladies in this episode,
most of their group, took to the road
until at last the group arrived
at Arthur's court where they contrived
to ask to have a favor granted
and have the king do as they wanted.
The king agreed before he knew*
what favor they would have him do; 5390
he'd grant whatever they required.
The ladies told him they desired
to have the queen, with his consent,
attend and watch their tournament.
He, never liking to refuse,
said he consented, did she choose.
The ladies as a group appeared
before the queen, immensely cheered,
and she immediately was told:
"My lady, please do not withhold 5400

[149]

our favor granted by the king."
The queen asked of the gathering:
"Do not conceal this boon; what is it?"
They told her: "If you wish to visit
and to attend our tournament,
he will raise no impediment
against it and will not contend."
The queen replied she would attend,
since he had given his permission.

5410   The maidens sent men upon a mission
to bear the message through the land
that, on the day that they had planned
to have the tournament convene,
the maids were going to bring the queen.
The news was carried everywhere,
both near and far and here and there,
and it became so widely spread
it finally reached the kingdom dread
from which once nobody returned,

5420   but these days anyone who yearned
could enter and could leave the land,
because it was no longer banned.
The news was thus disseminated
throughout the realm, retold, related,
until it reached a seneschal
of Meleagant, inimical,
the traitor who should burn in Hell!
The house wherein this man did dwell
held Lancelot, under arrest,

5430   at his foe Meleagant's behest,
who hated him with deadly hate.
When Lancelot had learned the date
and hour of the tournament
and was informed of the event,
tears filled his eyes, his heart was grieved.
The lady of the house perceived
that Lancelot was sad and pensive

and asked in private, apprehensive:
"My lord, by God and by your soul,
tell me the truth, as I cajole.   5440
You are so changed that now you shrink
from laughter and from food and drink;
diversion leaves you disinclined.
You can tell me what's on your mind
and what has made you so depressed."
"Ah lady, if I am distressed,
by God above, you should not wonder.
I am downcast and torn asunder
to think that I cannot be found
among the best the world around;   5450
a joust with everyone assembling,
so I believe without dissembling.
Yet, lady, if you do not mind,
if God made you so good and kind
that you would give me leave to go,
I would behave, you surely know,
so honorably toward you in turn
that to your prison I'd return."
"I would with pleasure, without fail,
if only it did not entail   5460
my own destruction and demise.
But I so fear and so despise,
Lord Meleagant contemptible,
I would not dare oppose his will;
he would annihilate my lord.
No wonder he is so abhorred;
he is as vicious as you know."
"My lady, if you're fearing so
that I, once that I leave the joust,
will not return where I am housed,   5470
there is an oath that I shall take,
a vow that I shall never break,
that nothing that may have arisen
will hinder my return to prison

right after this great tournament."
"My word," she said, "I shall consent
on one condition." "Lady, what?"
"That you will come back to this spot
you'll swear to me and give your word,
5480 and of your love I'll be assured."
She gave him this alternative.
"My lady, all I have to give
I'll give to you when I've returned."
"Now I can see that I am spurned,"
the lady said to him with laughter,
"and someone else must have been after,
have taken over, and commanded
the love from you that I demanded,
and yet, without the least disdain,
5490 I'll take whatever may remain,
and be contented anyhow.
Moreover I shall take your vow
you will behave without derision
and will return here to my prison."
So Lancelot, by the holy church,
took the oath of which she was in search:
he would unfailingly return.
The lady gave to him in turn
her own lord's weapons, which were red,
5500 and then his charger, spirited
and marvellously fair and strong.
He mounted, left, and rode along,
in armor of a lovely hue,
completely fresh and wholly new,
until he came to Worstede's bound.
He halted at that point and found
a lodging place outside the town
on which a gentleman would frown,
for it was small, and low, and base,
5510 but he would not stay anyplace
wherein he might be recognized.

Though many knights, elite and prized,
were in the castle walls amassed,
outside their number was surpassed;
so many started to arrive
for the queen's sake, not one in five
could have been lodged beneath a rafter;
for every one came seven after
who would not ever have been seen
save for the presence of the queen.   5520
For five entire leagues, all around,
the barons lodged and could be found
in their pavilion, lodge, or tent,
and noble maids and ladies went;
amazing numbers were revealed.
Now, Lancelot had hung his shield
outside upon his lodging door,
and, to relax his body more,
he had removed his arms and lain
upon a bed worth his disdain: 5530
a narrow bed, thin mattress stuff,
its hempen cover coarse and rough.
He lay, disarmed, unhelmeted,
stretched on his side upon this bed.
As he lay in such miseries,
a fellow came in his chemise,*
a herald-at-arms now bereft
of coat and shoes, which he had left
back at the tavern, unprotected
against the wind. When he detected   5540
the shield hung in the doorway there
he came up hurriedly, feet bare;
there was no way he could have known it
or known what knight might bear or own it.
He saw the house door open wide,
and so the herald went inside.
Upon the bed lay Lancelot.
The herald knew him on the spot,

and he began to cross himself.
5550   Lancelot looked across himself
and told him not to speak his name
in any place to which he came.
If he let what he knew escape,
he'd think himself in better shape
with one snapped neck or both eyes gored.
"I have esteemed you highly, lord,
I always have; be positive
that never, all the days I live,
will I, upon the least pretext.
5560   do anything to make you vexed."
The herald bounded from the dwelling
and went off oft and loudly telling:
"Now one has come to take their measure! *
Now one has come to take their measure!"
In every place that's what he cried.
The people leapt on every side
and asked the herald what he shouted.
He did not dare say whom he touted,
but kept repeating it instead,
5570   and this was when it was first said,
"Now one has come to take their measure!"
The herald used this cry with pleasure,
and taught us others this outburst;
our herald teacher said it first.
The parties gathered on the scene,
and all the ladies, and the queen,
and knights, and other folk besides,
and men-at-arms upon on all sides,
amassed to both the left and right.
5580   Erected at the tourney site
was an enormous wooden stand;
it was a structure that was planned
for the queen and maids and ladies there.
No one had seen a stand so fair,
so well constructed, or so long.

[154]

The following day, the entire throng
assembled and pursued the queen,
so they could watch the tourney scene
and learn the better and worse men.
The knights arrived there ten by ten,   5590
thirty by thirty, score by score,
eighty, ninety, one hundred, more,
and here two hundred in a band.
This huge crowd gathered around the stand,
so great a crowd for this event
that they began the tournament.
Unarmed and armed, the men assembled.
The lances that they bore resembled
a forest; those who liked such sporting
had such a lot they were transporting   5600
that nothing could be seen but lances,
banners and gonfalons' expanses.
The jousters moved on toward the joust
with many comrades they could roust
for jousting, where they were repairing,
and other people were preparing
for other feats of horsemanship.
The fields were so full, fallow strip
and plowed, no spectators could count
the knights, so vast was the amount.   5610
Now, this first gathering did not
include the fighter Lancelot,
who left his presence unrevealed,
but when he came across the field,
the herald noticed he came vying
and could not keep himself from crying,
"See who has come to take their measure!
See who has come to take their measure!"
"Who is this man?" asked all who heard.
The herald answered not a word.   5620
When Lancelot had made his entry,
of the elite he equalled twenty.*

He made so strong a start that day,
no one could take his eyes away,
wherever his skills he might employ.
There was a knight for Pomelegoi
whose nerve and valor were astounding;
his horse was galloping and bounding
like a wild stag, and full of fire.

5630 He was the son of the king of Eire
and was a splendid warrior,
but everyone liked four times more
the warrior who was unknown.
They wondered in an anxious tone,
"Who can be so well qualified?"
The queen discreetly drew aside
a maiden who was wise and fair
and told her: "Maiden, you must bear
a message for me in a trice;

5640 your words must be brief and concise.
From this wood stand you must alight;
on my behalf, go to that knight
who's carrying the shield of red,
and tell him privately I said
'Be worsted.' That is what I bid."
The maiden very promptly did
as the queen wanted, with discretion,
for she pursued the knight in question
until she was so very near,

5650 no bystanders could overhear.
In manner pleasant and serene,
she murmured, "Sir, my lady queen
sends me to give you this command.
So I would have you understand
you must 'be worsted.'" When he heard,
he said he willingly concurred,
as one who was entirely hers.
He rode against a knight, with spurs,
as fast as horse could bear him forward

and missed him when he should have scored.　　　5660
From then till evenfall was seen
he fought his worst to please the queen.
His knight assailant had not missed
but struck him blows hard to resist
and roughly pressed upon the knight.
At that point Lancelot took flight
and did not turn his horse's neck
against a knight he sought to check
again that day; were he to die,
his deeds would only mortify　　　5670
and cause him great disgrace and shame.
Of everyone who went and came
he made believe he was in fear.
The knights began to laugh and jeer
and made him be a butt of jest,
when once they had been much impressed.
The herald, who had once begun
to cry: "He'll beat them one by one,"
was mortified; the words he spoke
made him the butt of jest and joke.　　　5680
They said: "Now hush, friend, be at leisure;
this knight will take nobody's measure.
He measured till his yardstick broke!
So much for him of whom you spoke."
And several said: "What can this mean?
Just now he was so bold and keen,
and now the coward feels such fright
he will not wait for any knight.
Perhaps he was superior
because he'd not borne arms before;　　　5690
when he arrived he was so strong,
no knight could stand against him long,
however skilled at arms and seasoned;
he lashed out like a man unreasoned.
He's learned so much of arms and strife
that nevermore throughout his life

will he want to bear arms again.
His weak heart cannot stand the strain.
He must be the worst coward living."
The queen had not the least misgiving,
but was well pleased by his compliance,
for she knew well, and yet kept silence,
that he was truly Lancelot.
He let his cowardliness blot
his character all day till night,
but dusk suspended the great fight.
On parting, knights of more repute
became involved in a dispute.
The Irish king's son, on reflection,
believed there could be no objection:
his was all praise and his the prize,
but he was wrong in his surmise;
his equals there were plentiful.
The noblest and most beautiful
of maids and ladies all concurred
the red knight was whom they preferred.
They'd watched him more than anyone.
How well at first this knight had done
the ladies all had clearly seen.
First he was noble, bold of mien,
and after was so filled with fright
that he dared not attack a knight,
so all the worst, should they prefer,
could take the red knight prisoner
or strike him down as they collided.
But men and women all decided
they would return the next daybreak
to tourney, and the maids would take
the knights who garnered the awards
to be their husbands and their lords.
So they declared, and turned their faces,
and went back to their lodging places.
When they arrived where they were staying,

5700

5710

5720

5730

at several, people started saying:
"Where is the knight the most abased,
the worst, the lowest, most disgraced?
Where can he be? Where has he ridden?
Where has he gone? Where has he hidden?
Where has he gone? Where to pursue him?
It may be we shall never view him,   5740
for we know Cowardice has chased
the knight, who holds her so embraced
no man on earth could be less treasured.
A hundred thousand times more leisured
the coward than the brave, the fighter,
so our contempt is all the righter.
For Cowardice can bring release,
and she has kissed the knight in peace
and has deprived him of his essence.
Prowess would not show such quiescence   5750
or be so vile as to reside
in him or sit down at his side,
but Cowardice is uppermost;
she is reposing in a host
who serves her and so dotes upon her
that for her he would forfeit honor."
The gossips slandered him all night
and spread malicious tales and spite,
but often someone who defames
is viler than the ones he blames   5760
and worse than those whom he despises.
Everyone voiced his own surmises
and said whatever he pleased and dared.
At daybreak they were all prepared
and came back to the tournament.
The queen, and maids, and ladies went
into the stand with many a knight
who bore no arms and could not fight:
as captives they'd sustained a loss
or had resolved to take the cross.*   5770

They told the ladies, to be charming,
the most admired knights' way of arming.
Some of them said: "Do you behold
the knight who has the band of gold
on his red shield? The knight we pick
is Governal of Roderic.
Do you see the next fighter ride,
who on his shield's face, side by side,
has placed an eagle and a dragon?
5780   He is the son of the king of Aragon;
into this land that rider came
to win great honor and acclaim.
And see his neighbor, can you tell
the one who spurs and jousts so well,
on whose shield, in the half that's green,
a painted leopard can be seen,
with azure on the overplus?
He's Ignaures the Covetous,
and he is amorous and pleasant.
5790   And see the rider who bears pheasant
on his shield, painted beak to beak?
He's Coguillant of Mautirec.
See those nearby upon the course,
each riding on a dappled horse,
with golden shields, with lions gray?
Their shields are styled alike that way,
for one is named Semiramis,
the other's a comrade of his.
Now, see the knight who bears the weight
5800   of a shield painted with a gate,
so that it looks as if a deer
is going through? That's King Yder."
Up in the stand they would disclose:
"That shield was fashioned in Limoges
and brought back here by Pilades,
who always seeks with eagerness
to tourney and would not refuse.

The other was made in Toulouse
with harness straps and stirrups all;
it has been brought by Kay of Estral.   5810
That one's from Lyons on the Rhone,
none finer under Heaven's throne,
which Taulas of the Desert won
for a great service he had done.
He bears it well and is well covered.
This other shield will be discovered
of English work and London made,
on which two swallows are displayed,
both poised for flight; although they feel
many a blow from Poitevin steel,   5820
they do not move as blows are rung.
It's carried by Thoas the Young."
The knights gave such an overview
of arms borne by the men they knew
but did not see the weapons borne
by him whom they all held in scorn.
They thought that he must have retreated;
he had not joined them and competed
in the great tourney. When the queen
found he was nowhere to be seen,   5830
she wanted someone to be bound
to search the ranks till he was found
and could think of no better choice
than yesterday's to be her voice.
At once she called the maid to tell:
"Go mount your palfrey, mademoiselle.
I send you back where you were sent
to search throughout the tournament
and find the knight of yesterday.
Let nothing cause you to delay,   5840
and tell him, as you did before,
he must 'be worsted' one time more.
When you have told him to comply
pay closest heed to his reply."

The maiden did not tarry there.
Last evening she'd remarked with care
which way this warrior had sought,
so obviously the maiden thought
she would be sent another day.
5850 Down through the ranks she made her way
until she saw the knight discussed
and promptly told him that he must
"be worsted" in the jousting places,
would he enjoy the queen's good graces
and have her love; so she demanded.
He answered: "Since she has commanded,
please tell her I extend my thanks."
She left and went back through the ranks.
Youths, men-at-arms, and squires were near,
5860 and all of them began to jeer:
"See, wondrous things may be discerned;
the knight with red arms has returned.
What is he doing? On this earth
there is no man of lesser worth,
no man so vile and so misprized,
so cowardly and so despised,
for Cowardice has him in thrall;
there's nothing he can do at all."
The maiden came back to the queen,
5870 impatient for her go-between
to hear what words he would employ.
His answer gave her greatest joy,
because she knew that it was he,
the one whose she was totally,
and he was totally her own.
She told the maiden to make known
to him her order and request:
he was to do his "very best";
go back at once and tell him so.
5880 The maid replied that she would go;
without delay he would be found.

[162]

She came down from the stand to ground,
where lackeys of her own attended,
and took her palfrey, which they tended.
The maiden rode, when she was mounted,
and found the knight, and she recounted:
"Now, sir, my lady orders you
to do 'the best' that you can do."
He answered: "Now you say to her
nothing could cause me to demur,   5890
if she desires and thinks it right.
What pleases her gives me delight."
The maiden was not slow to bear
a message so extremely fair,
because she thought it would enchant
the queen and make her jubilant.
So as directly as she could
she went back to the stand of wood,
having this message to disclose.
The queen observed her and arose   5900
to meet her, but came to a stop
and waited at the stairway top,
so she did not descend its measure.
The maid arrived with greatest pleasure
to give the message in her care,
and she began to climb the stair.
She told her, when she reached the queen:
"My lady, I have never seen
a knight so fine in speech and form
who is so willing to perform   5910
whatever you command him do,
and, if you ask me what is true,
he's equally disposed, at will,
both to do well and to do ill."
"My word," she said, "that may well be."
She went back to the sill to see
the knights as she had done before.
And Lancelot delayed no more;

[163]

by the arm-straps he seized his shield.
5920   He burned to have his nerve revealed
and all his prowess without check.
Lancelot turned his horse's neck
and let him run between two rows.
Soon they would be amazed, all those
derisory, deluded folk
who'd made him be a jest and joke
a good part of the day and night.
Long had they sported with delight
and had made fun of his mishaps.
5930   With his arm placed through his shield straps
the Irish king's son spurred to ride
upon him from the other side,
and after the two knights collided,
the king of Ireland's son decided
the tournament no longer mattered,
for his lance snapped apart and shattered,
so it became a total loss,
because he had not struck on moss
but on a shield face, hard and dry.
5940   Lancelot taught how to apply
one of his master strokes of harm:
he knocked his shield right off his arm
and pressed his arm against his side
and, from the horse he was astride,
he threw the king's son to the ground.
From both sides knights spurred, lunging, bound
some to cut off the ruler's son,
some to see Lancelot undone
and help their lord as he competed.
5950   Most of them promptly were unseated
during the tournament and fray,
but not one time throughout the day
were weapons fingered by Gawain,
for he decided to refrain,
because he so enjoyed the sight

of the great skill shown by the knight
with red arms as he was assailed;
he found the deeds of others paled.
Gawain was with the others there
but felt that they could not compare. 5960
The herald then began to call,
so that he could be heard by all,
and cried aloud with greatest pleasure:
"The man has come to take their measure!
What he can do will now be known!
Today his prowess will be shown!"
Lancelot turned his horse and spurred
toward a brave knight, and he conferred
a blow that knocked him on the course
one hundred feet from his war horse. 5970
Then he began to handle lance
and sword with so much elegance
that every man who had been armed
watched him employ them and was charmed.
Many of those with arms to bear
were highly pleased and thought it fair,
because it was great sport indeed
to see how he made knight and steed
together stagger in their tracks
and crumple under his attacks. 5980
Few of the knights he chanced to meet
were able to retain their seat,
and he bestowed the steeds he won
on everyone who wanted one.
Then those who had been jeering said:
"We are disgraced and shamed and dead.
We were extremely ill-advised
to have disparaged and despised
this knight, for it has been revealed
he's worth a thousand on this field. 5990
He's conquered and surpassed in worth
all knights that can be found on earth.

Not one of them could be his match."
Maids called him marvellous to watch;
none stood a chance to be his bride.
On wealth and beauty none relied,
nor on position or high birth,
for loveliness and monied worth
the knight disdained in choice of wife.
6000   He'd proved himself so brave in strife
that he would not have any maid.
Yet many vows like these were made:
could they not wed this chevalier
they would not marry in this year
or give themselves as a reward
to any husband, any lord.
The queen, who heard them overstating
their viewpoints and exaggerating,
laughed silently and mockingly.
6010   Were all the gold in Araby,
as she well knew, before him spread,
the fairest maid and highest bred
would not be his, were she the best,
the one desired by all the rest.
The maidens all, of one accord,
each sought to have him as her lord.
There was such jealousy and strife,
each maiden might have been his wife.
They saw how skillfully he fought,
6020   and none of them believed or thought
another knight, though he might please,
could equal his abilities.
He fought so well that, when he went,
on both sides of the tournament
they all declared without a lie
that no knight at the joust could tie
with him who bore the shield of red.
But when he went away, he shed
shield, lance, and horsecloth, and allowed

[166]

his gear to fall amidst the crowd   6030
where everyone was bunched most thickly,
and then he turned and rode off quickly.
So Lancelot rode off dissembling,
and no one in the crowd assembling
took notice that he had departed.
To reach the place from where he started
Lancelot took to the road
and went straight back to the abode
in his sworn word's accomplishment.
As people left the tournament,   6040
all asked for him, but they could not
find any trace of Lancelot,
for he had fled them while disguised,
not wanting to be recognized.
The knights were grief-stricken and pained;
they'd have rejoiced if he'd remained.
If Lancelot's resolve to leave
had caused the other knights to grieve,
when the maids learned that it was so
they suffered even greater woe,   6050
and, by Saint John, they made it clear
they would not marry in this year.
Since their first choice was not permitted,
they left the others uncommitted.
The tourney ended with adieus;
no husbands did the maidens choose.
Now Lancelot, without delay,
returned to prison straightaway.
Two or three days before he came
the seneschal returned the same   6060
and asked where Lancelot might be.
The lady, who had splendidly
equipped him with red arms at need
and furnished harness and a steed,
went to the steward and admitted
the truth of how she had outfitted

their prisoner, whom she had sent
to joust at Worstede tournament.
She told the truth about it all.
6070 "My lady," said the seneschal,
"you could not have done any worse.
Misfortune may well be my curse:
Lord Meleagant, who's far from pliant,
will treat me worse than would the giant *
if I were shipwrecked in the sea,
and I shall die in agony.
When he learns Lancelot attended,
no clemency will be extended."
"My lord, do not be so dismayed,"
6080 the lady said, "or so afraid;
it is extremely unbecoming.
Nothing will hinder him from coming;
he swore on relics to make good
his word and come back once he could."
At once the seneschal remounted,
went to his liege lord, and recounted
the whole adventure and affair,
but told him how his wife took care
that Lancelot had pledged his word,
6090 so his lord would be reassured.
"I know well that he would be loath
to break faith and betray his oath,"
responded Meleagant, "and yet
your wife has caused me deep regret.
He'd never have had my consent
to travel to that tournament.
You must ride back now and take heed,
when he returns as he agreed,
that Lancelot will be confined
6100 within a prison of a kind
against which he cannot prevail;
his body powerless in jail.
Inform me when he is at hand."

[168]

"It shall be done as you command,"
the steward said. He left and learned
that Lancelot had now returned
to his court as a prisoner.
The steward had a messenger
to Meleagant run to report
that Lancelot had reached his court.   6110
Then Meleagant, once he had heard
that Lancelot had kept his word,
assembled carpenter and mason,
willing or under obligation,
so they would follow his command.
He found the finest in the land
and ordered them to build a tower
and labor hard, with all their power,
till it was built not far from Gorre
with stone brought over sea to shore.   6120
There was an isle he knew to be
in a broad inlet of the sea;
to Meleagant it was well known.
He ordered them to ship the stone,
and cut down lumber, and to raise
the tower; in fifty-seven days
or less, the tower was complete:
a strong and solid, tall retreat.
After the tower had been founded,
within it Meleagant impounded   6130
Lancelot, who was in his power.

LANCELOT'S IMPRISONMENT

E placed him by night in the tower,*
had the doors walled, the knight immured,
and all the masons he adjured
to swear that they would never say

[169]

one word about it any day.
He sought to have the tower concealed
without an entrance left unsealed
except one window, which was small.
6140   So Lancelot, within the wall,
had to remain in solitude.
They gave him scant and wretched food
at scheduled hours of repast;
through that small window food was passed,
the way that treacherous, underhanded
villain directed and commanded.
Then Meleagant, who had succeeded
in all that he desired, proceeded
directly to King Arthur's court.
6150   Once he arrived there to report
before King Arthur, Meleagant,
most treacherous and arrogant,
began his speechmaking by telling:
"King, in your presence and your dwelling
I set a battle but do not
see any sign of Lancelot,
who vowed to be my adversary.
Yet, as it is deemed necessary,
I challenge him, when all can hear,
6160   before the people who are here.
If he is here, let him step out
and say that we shall have our bout
in your court one year from today.
If you've been told about the way
it was arranged that we would fight,
I do not know, but in my sight
are knights to witness to the fact;
knights present when we made our pact
who'll tell it for your benefit,
6170   if they choose to acknowledge it.
If Lancelot seeks to deny me,
no mercenary need I buy me;

I shall ensure he is corrected."
At the king's side the queen directed
the king to lean over and began:
"Sire, do you recognize that man?
It's he who carried me away
when I was led by steward Kay.
The man is Meleagant by name,
and he caused Kay much harm and shame."　　　　6180
"Lady," the king said to the queen,
"I understand all that you mean.
He is the one who a long while
detained my people in exile."
The queen left her thoughts unexpressed.
To Meleagant the king addressed
his words and the reply he made:
"My friend, may Heaven grant me aid,
no news of Lancelot was brought,
and we are saddened and distraught."　　　　6190
So Meleagant resumed his tale:
"But Lancelot said without fail
that I would locate him here, sire.
I'm not permitted to require
our combat elsewhere than your court.
I want these barons to report
that they all can give evidence
I summon him here one year hence
according to the solemn plight
we made when we agreed to fight." *　　　　6200
The lord Gawain rose at that word,
extremely grieved by what he'd heard.
"Sir, Lancelot, we understand,
cannot be found throughout this land.
We'll have more territory covered.
God willing, he will be discovered
before one year ends, without fail,
if he is not slain or in jail.
If he does not appear, assign

[171]

6210   the fight to me; let it be mine.
I'll arm myself for Lancelot
if he has not come to this spot
upon that day one year from now."
"Ah ha! God, good king, do allow
what he desires and what I want,
I beg of you," said Meleagant.
"Throughout the world I know no knight
against whom I would test my might
as willingly, save Lancelot.

6220   But do be sure, if I do not
fight either knight of such repute
I shall accept no substitute.
One of these two is my condition."
The king told him he had permission,
if Lancelot were not to come.
Then Meleagant departed from
the court presided by King Arthur
and rode until he found his father,
King Bademagu, without repose.

6230   Before him he began to pose,
attempting to appear elated,
so that he would be highly rated
and would seem prominent and bold.
That day was when the king would hold
in Bath, his city, joyous court.
It was his birthday; every sort
of person went there and attended,
and so the court was full and splendid
with those who came to be with him.

6240   The palace was filled to the brim
with many a knight and demoiselle.
Of one maid I shall later tell
my thinking and my comprehension,
but of her now I make no mention,
preferring rather to resist her
(for she was Meleagant's own sister),

because it would be out of place,
and I intend, not to deface
my narrative or to distort it
by being too quick to report it,   6250
to follow on a straight good road.
I'll tell you the next episode
at once, how Meleagant came near
and when all, great and small, could hear,
he spoke up: "Father, God save you,
and, if you please, now tell me true,"
he asked his sire in a loud voice,
"has not a man grounds to rejoice
and think that he should be revered,
once that his weapons make him feared   6260
before King Arthur's royal court?"
The father promptly cut him short
and made his answer understood.
"My son," he said, "all who are good
ought to be honoring and serving
a man who was proved so deserving
and want to keep him company."
And so the king used flattery
and asked his son not to conceal
why he spoke thus and to reveal   6270
his wishes and from whence he came.
Meleagant started to proclaim:
"Sire, I don't know if you recall
the terms and the agreements all
that were both spoken and recorded
when by your pains we were accorded,
and Lancelot and I were checked.
I think that you will recollect
that both of us were to appear
at Arthur's court after one year;   6280
so we were told before a crowd.
I went to court when I had vowed,
outfitted with accoutrement,

[173]

prepared for that for which I went,
and did exactly as I ought.
For Lancelot I asked and sought,
with whom I was to stand my ground,
but he was nowhere to be found.
He had eluded me and fled.
6290 I left court when Gawain had said
that he would pledge his word and vow,
if Lancelot's not living now
or otherwise fails to appear
within the limit of one year,
that no postponement will there be,
and he himself will fight with me
for Lancelot and in his stead.
No knight of Arthur's can be said
as praiseworthy, so all presume;
6300 before the elderberries bloom
I shall discern from our attacks
whether his fame squares with the facts.
I wish that now we two could fight."
"Son," said the sire, "to speak aright,
you're acting like an idiot,
and anyone who knew it not
has learned your folly straight from you.
A noble heart is humble, true;
it is the fool and the stiff-necked
6310 whose foolishness cannot be checked.
My son, your nature is so sere,
I say, so harsh and so severe,
it has no friendliness or kindness.
With you compassion meets with blindness;
your foolishness is never finished,
and I consider you diminished,
and that is what will bring you down.
If you are brave and of renown,
so many will attest to it
6320 when the time comes and it is fit.

A worthy man would never need
to praise his nerve to gild his deed;
the deed will utter its own praise.
Self-adulation does not raise
your standing, but it makes me deem
that you deserve far less esteem.
I scold you, son, but what's the use?
To words a fool remains obtuse.
One tires oneself without success
in ridding him of foolishness,   6330
and wisdom, though taught and supplied,
is worthless if it's not applied,
and lost and vanished in a hurry."
Then Meleagant was wild with fury.
In truth no man of mother born
was ever seen as filled with scorn
as he was, I would have you know.
So violent did his anger grow
that peace between the two was broken,
for he was in no way soft-spoken   6340
but told his father: "Are you dreaming?
Is this a nightmare, with you deeming
that I am totally insane,
when I endeavor to explain
my life to you and what I do?
I thought that I could come to you
as to my lord, as to my father.
It seems to me I should not bother,
for the abuse that you reserve
for me is worse than I deserve.   6350
I think so, and you cannot say
why you've begun to speak this way."
"I can indeed." "What may it be?"
"There's nothing in you that I see
but madness, rage, and turpitude.
I know your temperament and mood,
and they will yet cause you to grieve.

[175]

Cursed be whoever would believe
that Lancelot, that splendid knight,
6360   for fear of you would take to flight,
for all but you believe him brave.
He may be buried in his grave
or else within some prison, locked
behind a door so tightly blocked
he cannot leave without permission.
To learn he was in that position:
if he were dead or in such dire
straits would fill me full of ire.
Indeed, the loss would be untold
6370   if one so handsome and so bold,
yet so fair-minded, and so skilled,
should prove to be untimely killed,
but that, God willing, is a lie."
Bademagu ceased his reply,
but everything he had related
was overheard when it was stated
by a young daughter of the king,
the maiden I was mentioning
previously when she appeared
6380   in my tale. Now she heard, uncheered,
such news of Lancelot revealed.
She knew he must be kept concealed,
to disappear without a trace.
She said, "God never see my face,
if I take rest while I pursue
news that's reliable and true."
The moment that she had the notion,
not causing one bit of commotion,
the maiden ran to get astride
6390   a handsome mule that she could ride,
which had a very easy gait.
But for my part I shall relate
she did not know which way to go.*
When she left court, she did not know

or ask which way she should be bound.
She traveled the first road she found
and rode with great precipitance,
not knowing which way, but by chance,
without a man-at-arms or knight.
She hurried, longing so to sight   6400
the object of her swift pursuit,
and how she searched on every route,
but was not soon to end her quest,
in one location long to rest,
or think of pausing for repose,
if she sought a successful close
once she'd embarked on her decision:
releasing Lancelot from prison
if she could locate and unbind him.
I think before the maid could find him   6410
she had to search in many lands,
on many roads and many strands
before she had some information.
Why should I feel an obligation
to tell her overnights and days?
The maiden rode down many ways,
up hill, down dale, below and high,
till over one month had passed by,
and still the maid knew nothing more
or less than she had known before,   6420
and was completely at a loss.
Then one day, as she rode across
a meadow, pensive and heartsore,
far off upon an inlet shore
she saw a tower, but there was not
within a league's range of the spot
a house or dwelling or a hut.
Meleagant had it built and shut
Lancelot within its wall,
and she knew none of it at all.   6430
Once she saw where the tower was raised,

[177]

the maiden stared at it, and gazed,
and could not take away her eyes.
Her own heart made her realize
it was what she had long pursued,
what she had wanted had ensued,
and Fortune* led her the right way
who had long led her far astray.
She neared the tower on the strand
6440   till she could touch it with her hand.
She went around it with ear bent
and listened, totally intent.
Perhaps she'd hear a sound or voice
to give her reason to rejoice.
The base and summit she espied
and saw the tower was tall and wide.
The maiden wondered all the more
there was no window and no door
except one window, close and small.
6450   To reach the tower, straight and tall,
there was no ladder and no stair.
She thought it had been planned with care
with Lancelot therein confined,
and thus the maid, before she dined,
would learn if it were true or not.
She wanted to call Lancelot;
she wanted to call him by name
but tarried longer, all the same,
and while she had not said a word,
6460   within the wondrous tower, she heard
a voice lamenting, spending breath
on words that only longed for death.
He coveted his death; he grieved;
his suffering was unrelieved.
He wished to die and end his strife;
he loathed his body and his life
and made a weak and hoarse appeal.
"Ah, Fortune, you have turned your wheel

[178]

appallingly to change my case:
once at the peak, now at the base;   6470
once so well off, now I'm reviled,
and now you weep when once you smiled.
Alas, poor wretch, why had you placed
such trust in her, when in such haste
she vanished, leaving you for lost!
In no time Fortune had me tossed
from such high to such low degree.
Oh, Fortune, when you toyed with me
you wronged me, but what do you care?
You're unconcerned with how we fare.   6480
Ah! Holy Spirit, Holy Cross!
Now I am doomed and at a loss,
and I am not long for this earth.
Alas! Gawain, such is your worth,
that no one else can be so kind.
It is a wonder to my mind
you have not ridden to my aid!
You surely have been long delayed
and are not acting courteously.
A friend you so loved previously   6490
should be entitled to your care.
Unfailingly I can declare
on either shore the sea embraces
I'd search in all secluded places
just to ensure you were released
for seven years or ten, at least,
until my efforts had availed,
if I had learned that you were jailed.
But why indulge in idle chatter?
It's clear to me I do not matter   6500
enough for you to care to make
the effort needed for my sake.
The peasants rightfully contend
how hard it is to find one friend.
It's easy in adversity

[179]

to learn who your real friends may be.
Alas! I've spent more than one year
imprisoned in this tower here.
To leave me here, Gawain, was low,
6510 but possibly you did not know,
and it is wrong of me to blame you.
I'm sure it's true and I defame you
to think that's what you'd have allowed.
By everything that's capped by cloud,
if the true facts had been presented,
nothing would ever have prevented
your men and you from the assignment
of freeing me from my confinement
by coming to this place of woe.
6520 You would be bounden to do so
as my companion and my friend.
I would not otherwise contend,
but help I uselessly importune.
As for the cause of such misfortune,
alas, by God and Saint Silvester,
God grant that he may also fester.
Malicious Meleagant be cursed!
Of living men he is the worst
and does the worst to me he can."
6530 This outburst calmed and stilled the man
whose life was spent in suffering.
Below the maid was lingering.
When she heard all he had to say
she would not tarry or delay.
She knew she'd reached the proper spot
and sensibly called "Lancelot"
as loudly as she had the power.
"My friend, you up there in the tower,
speak to one of your friends down here."
6540 The man within it did not hear.
She shouted louder at some length,
until the man who had no strength

could hear her call and was amazed.
He wondered whose voice was upraised.
He heard the voice call out his name,
but did not know from where it came,
and thought a phantom must have cried.
He looked around himself and tried
to see a stranger's face or limb
but only saw the tower and him.   6550
"Lord," he exclaimed, "what do I hear?
Talk when I see nobody near!
What makes it even more breathtaking
is I am not asleep but waking.
If, dreaming, I had heard the cry
I might believe it was a lie,
but I am wakeful and concerned."
With effort he arose and turned
and went to the small window there,
little by little, taking care.   6560
Over the sill he leaned his head,
looked high and low and straight ahead
with greatest care and to the side
until, as he looked out, he spied
the maid who shouted from below,
though who she was he did not know.
She recognized him all the same
and told him: "Lancelot, I came
in search of you from far away,
and things have happened in a way   6570
that I have found you, thank the Lord.
When you went toward the Bridge of the Sword,
I am the one who said I wanted
a favor of you, which you granted
most willingly when I entreated:
the head of the knight you defeated,
whom I had you decapitate,
for whom I felt tremendous hate.
This service was so generous,

[181]

6580 my efforts have been strenuous
to find and get you out of here."
"My gratitude is most sincere,
and for the service I accorded
I shall be very well rewarded,"
in turn the prisoner replied,
"if I can make my way outside.
If you can get me out somehow,
then I can truly say and vow
my debt to you will be colossal,
6590 so help me Saint Paul the Apostle,
and if I see God in the face,
I'll do your bidding with good grace,
and I shall be your man forever.
Maid, any possible endeavor
that you could ask me to essay
shall be performed without delay."
"My dear friend, let your doubting cease;
this is the day of your release.
I shall not fail on any grounds,
6600 not even for a thousand pounds,
to free you by the break of day.
Then I shall give you a long stay,
much rest, and everything to ease you.
Whatever I have that may please you,
ask, and it will not be refused.
You will not be the least ill-used.
Now I must search for some device
within this land that will suffice,
wherever such I can procure,
6610 for widening this aperture
until you make your way outside."
To that the prisoner replied,
for he was of the selfsame mind:
"Such tool may Heaven let you find.
Within the tower I have some rope
the men-at-arms gave me to cope

with hauling up meals nauseating
to stomach and debilitating:
hard barley bread and brackish water."
Thereon Bademagu's young daughter   6620
found a stout pickaxe, sharp and strong,★
which she immediately passed along.
At once he pounded and attacked
the window with the blows he whacked;
although they left him worn and spent,
he soon escaped imprisonment.
Then he was very much relieved
and joyous, as may be believed,
when his release had been secured
from where he was so long immured.   6630
He was at large and uncontrolled,
and do believe, for all the gold
dispersed throughout the wide world's sweep,
amassed, and piled high in a heap,
and offered him to take or spurn,
that nevermore would he return.
So Lancelot escaped this way,
so feeble he began to sway
with weakness and decrepitude.
The maiden, with solicitude,   6640
so he would not be hurt or sore,
put him upon her mule before,
and at high speed away they rode.
The maiden chose back way and road
so they would not be seen but hidden,
for if they openly had ridden,
whoever found and recognized them
might well have harmed or brutalized them,
and that the maiden would not face.
So she avoided each bad place   6650
and reached a dwelling, fine and fair,
where she would frequently repair,
a pleasing home of elegance.

[183]

The dwelling and inhabitants
obeyed her orders and decisions.
Within were plenty of provisions,
and it was healthful and secluded.
There Lancelot's mule ride concluded.
As soon as he came through the door,
6660 the maid removed the clothes he wore,
and gently placed his frame and head
upon a high and lovely bed,
and bathed and cared for Lancelot
so very well that I cannot
describe or tell you half of it.
Her handling was every bit
as gentle as she would have cared
for her own father. She repaired,
restored, and made him a new man.
6670 He was not feeble, starved, and wan,
as he had been upon his freeing,
but handsome as an angel being.
So, strong and handsome, he arose.
The maiden sent for pleasing clothes,
the finest robe that she possessed.
When he arose he was so dressed.
He donned the clothes, his heart more light
than if it were a bird in flight.
He kissed and hugged the demoiselle.*
6680 "My friend, that I am hale and well
is thanks to God and you alone,"
he told her in a pleasant tone,
"Because of you I'm out of prison;
of my belongings and provision,
my body, service, and my heart,
whatever you please, take any part.
You've helped me so, I am your own.
My liege lord Arthur, though, has shown
great honor toward me; at his court
6690 I've long neglected to report,

[184]

and there I've many things to do.
For love, I ask you, and I sue
for leave to go there; I entreat
my friend, so gentle and so sweet,
for I would willingly attend."
"Dear Lancelot, beloved friend,
you may," the maiden said, agreeing.
"I seek your honor and well-being
above all else, both here and there."
The maiden had a wondrous, fair   6700
charger, the best seen she kept.
She gave it to him, and he leapt,
not touching stirrups on his bound,
upon it he was swiftly found.
Each prayed the other could rely
on God, who never tells a lie.

THE LAST BATTLE

LANCELOT took to the road
so glad no record that I owed
on oath of his joy would be apt,
at his escape when he was trapped.   6710
He often silently repeated:
cursed be the traitor who maltreated
and held him prisoner, encased,
whose lineage he had disgraced
by the misdeed he had committed,
and who was tricked now and outwitted.
"Despite him I got out of there!"
With heart and body he did swear,
by Him who made the whole world round,
that not for all the riches found   6720
twixt Babylon and Ghent's landscape
would he let Meleagant escape,

[185]

if he could gain the upper hand
and place his foe at his command;
his shame and treatment had been dread.
The case was coming to a head;
soon he would find the miscreant,
because that very Meleagant
he threatened that he would repay
6730 had come to Arthur's court that day,
though not at anyone's behest.
When he arrived, his first request
was to see Sir Gawain, and later,
when they had met, the proven traitor
inquired: was Lancelot around?
had he been sighted or been found?
as if he were quite ignorant.
He was in part, but Meleagant
thought he had each and every fact.
6740 Gawain told him what was exact
of Lancelot: he could report
he'd not been seen or come to court.
"Since I have found you anyhow,"
said Meleagant, "come keep your vow.
I will no longer be kept waiting."
Gawain replied unhesitating:
"God willing, on whom I rely,
soon both of us will start to vie.
I'll keep my promise in a trice,
6750 but as if we were playing dice,
and I'd more points than you enjoy,
so help me Heaven and Saint Foy,
before you cease to be beset
I shall win each and every bet."
Gawain, without delaying more,
ordered a carpet spread before
his feet, and he was unopposed.
Immediately the squires, composed,
did as commanded by Gawain

[186]

and did not grumble or complain.   6760
They did his bidding with good grace.
They laid the carpet in the place
he ordered that it should be kept.
Without a pause, on it he leapt.
An order to be armed he spoke
to youths who did not wear a cloak
and stood before him. There were three:
cousins or nephews, as may be,
I don't know their degree of nearness,
but they were expert, bold, and fearless.   6770
They armed him well, so well in fact
that there was nothing that he lacked.
There was no fault that could be found
by any man the world around,
they were so very competent.
When they had armed Gawain, one went
to fetch a steed that came from Spain,
on hill and dale and wood and plain
his pace was more precipitous
than that of good Bucephalus.*   6780
Upon this horse that I've recounted
Gawain, distinguished knight, was mounted,
the most experienced and fine
that ever made the cross' sign.
He was about to seize his shield
then saw, dismounting on the field,
Lancelot. He did not expect him.
and was astonished to detect him,
he came so suddenly and fast.
Gawain's amazement was as vast,   6790
I tell you, and I do not lie,
as if he'd fallen from the sky,
and yet there was no self-deception
about Gawain or his perception,
for it was Lancelot indeed,
and he dismounted from his steed.

With outstretched arms he reached the place
to greet his friend with an embrace,
which nothing there could have prevented.
6800 Gawain was joyful and contented
that his companion had been found.
I'll tell you proven truth and sound,
if you will put your faith in me:
Gawain would have refused to be
elected king upon the spot
if he could not have Lancelot.
The king knew, everybody knew it,
that Lancelot, whoever might rue it,
who'd been awaited for so long,
6810 was back among them hale and strong.
Together all expressed elation;
the court amassed for celebration;
they'd waited for him a long while.
There was none, aged or juvenile,
not one without a joyous face.
Rejoicing managed to efface
the sorrow that had persevered.
So mourning fled and joy appeared,
and eagerly joy called them there.
6820 What of the queen, now did she share
the joy by which all were engrossed?
Indeed she did; she was foremost.
What? Lord, where else would be the queen?
She'd never felt a joy as keen
as she now felt on his return;
would she not come to him in turn?
She had, and she was so close by
her body almost made a try
to follow her heart. Was it missing?
6830 Where was the queen's heart? It was kissing
and was caressing Lancelot.
Why did her body hide the thought?
Was it not wholly overjoyed?

Did it feel hateful and annoyed?
No, it had no such attitude.
It could be in that multitude
the king and others who were there
would have perceived the whole affair,
because their eyes were open wide.
She yearned to act, while people spied,   6840
upon this foolish, crazy thought,
an impulse that her heart so sought,
with which her Reason'd have no dealings,
for everyone would see her feelings.
What folly if they were exposed!
So Reason fettered and enclosed
her foolish heart and preferences.
The queen came somewhat to her senses
and put the matter to one side,
until the time she'd seen and spied   6850
a good and private place at court,
where they would have a safer port
than at the moment was their lot.
King Arthur honored Lancelot
and told him, when he had rejoiced:
"My friend, I have not heard news voiced
of any man for a long spell
I was as glad to hear them tell
as news of you. I long to learn
the country of your long sojourn;   6860
my curiosity is strong.
All winter and all summer long
I had them seek you high and low;
where you might be no one could show."
Said Lancelot: "Sire, in a word
I can explain what has occurred.
So briefly, what befell me later:
this Meleagant, this evil traitor,
has kept me as his prisoner
from the time when the prisoners were   6870

[189]

released in his land; since that hour,
beside the sea within a tower
he's made me live shamed and disgraced.
There he had me enclosed and placed.
My suffering would not be ended,
except that I have been befriended.
A friend of mine became my savior.
I once did her a little favor,
and for a tiny boon the maid

6880   gave a tremendous boon in trade,
the good and honor both were great.
But Meleagant, a man I hate,
who has afflicted and disgraced me,
and persecuted me, and chased me,
I am most eager to repay
immediately, without delay.
He should have that for which he came
and wait no more to press his claim.
He's more than ready; so am I.

6890   May Heaven grant that when we vie
he is not happy with his lot."
Gawain observed to Lancelot:
"This payment, friend; it would be better
if I were to repay your debtor.
A tiny boon it would be counted;
what's more, I am already mounted
and all prepared, as you can see.
Dear friend, don't keep this boon from me."
But Lancelot in his reply

6900   said that he would allow one eye
or even two plucked from his head
before he'd do as his friend said.
He swore Gawain would never sway him.
He owed his foe and would repay him,
for he had pledged it with his hand.
Gawain could clearly understand
no words of his would hold him back.

He took his hauberk off his back
and totally disarmed himself.
With these arms Lancelot armed himself   6910
without a moment of delay.
The hour he would be quits and pay
he had believed would never come
and found the waiting burdensome.
He could not rest till he was quits.
Meleagant nearly lost his wits
with his amazement and surprise
at what he saw with his own eyes
and was beside himself to find,
so that he nearly lost his mind.   6920
He said: "Oh, what a fool was I
to come here and not verify
this trickster was still in my power
within my prison in my tower.
Why would I have gone, Heaven knows?
What reason had I to suppose
he ever could have gotten out?
Are not the walls well built and stout;
the tower a strong and lofty vault?
There was no opening or fault   6930
he could have passed through to evade,
unless he had some outside aid.
Did word get out? Have stone walls crumbled?
Have they eroded till they tumbled?
But if the walls collapsed and fell,
would he not fall with them as well
and be dismembered, crushed, and dead?
Yes, Heaven help me, as I've said,
he would have died of such a fall.
Ere the collapse of that strong wall   6940
the sea would be dried up and sere,
so not a droplet would appear;
the world would not be in its course
unless it gave way under force.

[191]

That did not happen, I've no doubt,
and he had help when he got out.
He could not otherwise have flown.
Someone betrayed me, unbeknown.
However, he got out of there.

6950   If I had taken greater care,
he would have had no last resort
and never would have come to court,
but it is too late to repent.
The peasant, one who has no bent
for lies, says truly on this score
it is too late to lock the door*
with the horse stolen from the stable.
I realize, if I am not able
to suffer and to persevere,

6960   the shame and pain will be severe.
What suffering must I endure?
If it please God, in whom I'm sure,
I'll struggle not to be surpassed
and do my best while I can last."
At that point Meleagant revealed
how much he longed to share the field,
for he became adventuresome.
It seems to me the time had come,
for Lancelot desired to meet him,

6970   expecting swiftly to defeat him.
Before each knight assailed his foe,
the king directed each to go
before the tower on a moor.
In Ireland none had such allure.
Onto the moor the fighters wended
their way at once; as they descended,
the king went down with all the groups
of men and women in large troops.
They all went; none remained behind,

6980   and at the windows were aligned
the ladies, knights, and maidens there,

for Lancelot, wellborn and fair.
On the moor was a sycamore;*
its beauty was superior.
It took up space as it abounded,
and its vast tree trunk was surrounded
by lawn, fresh, lovely, and green-hued.
Its growth was constantly renewed.
Beneath this sycamore, sublime
and planted back in Abel's time,   6990
a clear spring flowed at rapid pace.
Its bed of stones had beauty, grace,
and shimmered with a silver gleam.
As for its pipe, so it would seem,
it was of gold, refined and pure.
The spring flowed down across the moor
between two woods and through a vale.
There was no troublesome detail;
the king was pleased to sit down there,
for everything he saw was fair.   7000
He told his people to stand back,
and Lancelot launched his attack
on Meleagant with the unabated
fury of one who deeply hated.
Before he struck at Meleagant,
he shouted, loud and adamant:
"Come here, I challenge you, I dare you;
and know that I shall never spare you;
of that you may be sure indeed!"
Then Lancelot spurred on his steed,   7010
drew back a little from the place,
about one bow's range to gain space.
Then each ran toward the other one
as swiftly as his horse could run.
Each struck the other on the field
upon his stout and sturdy shield.
The shields were pierced through by the blow,
but neither fighter harmed his foe

[193]

or pierced his flesh upon that try.
7020 They swiftly passed each other by,
then turned as fast as horse could run,
and struck hard blows, when they had spun,
upon the strong shields they employed.
Great were the efforts they deployed,
knights who were bold and of account,
each with a strong and speedy mount.
Tremendous blows the knights applied
on shields they held fast at the side.
Straight through the shields the lances hit,
7030 because they were not smashed or split,
and so they forced their way on in
until they reached their naked skin.
They pressed with the great strength they found
until both men were on the ground.
Each found his breast-strap, stirrups, girth
would prove to be of little worth;
each lost his seat with that hard blow
and fell back to bare ground below.
The horses were alarmed by it,
7040 and one mount bucked, the other bit;
each charger sought to make a kill,
then both ran off down dale, up hill.
The knights who'd fallen to the ground,
when they could, made an upward bound
and drew their swords, which were engraved
with letters. As the warriors braved
each other with their shields upraised,
from this point onward they appraised
the way they could begin to deal
7050 bad wounds with swords of sharpened steel.
But Lancelot felt no dismay,
with greater knowledge of swordplay
by half than Meleagant compiled,
for he had learned it as a child.
The knights applied hard, heavy blows

to shields they held to their sides, close,
and to their helms, which were gold-plated
and soon split and disintegrated,
but Lancelot would not relent;
the blow he struck was violent.   7060
He struck behind shield and enarme
on Meleagant's iron-clad right arm,
and slashed on down and severed it.
When Meleagant felt he was hit
on his right arm, which he had lost,
he said he'd sell it at high cost,
and if a chance came to attack,
nothing would tempt him to hold back,
because he felt such rage and pain
he very nearly went insane   7070
and thought the worst of his concern
could he not do him some bad turn.
To get his foe he rushed him hard,
but Lancelot was on his guard.
With his good sword he lacerated
his foe, whom he eviscerated,
which Meleagant would not outlast
till May and April came and passed.
He smashed the noseplate in his teeth
and broke three teeth off underneath.   7080
In Meleagant such fury flared,
he could not speak nor deigned be spared.
His heart, as false as it could be,
which was opposed to clemency,
left him imprisoned and encased.
Then Lancelot came and unlaced
his helmet and cut off his head.
That was his end; he fell down dead.
He would trick Lancelot no more.
I tell you that no spectator   7090
who was around the place would want
compassion shown to Meleagant.

King Arthur there, and all the rest,
felt greatest joy, which they expressed.
Those who were gladdest at his lot
removed the arms of Lancelot
and bore him off with greatest joy.

Lords, any more words I employ
would only come as an intrusion,
7100   so I am reaching the conclusion.
This is the ending of the work.
Though Godefroy de Leigny, clerk,⋆
has put the last hand to The Cart,
no blame to him should one impart;
he wrote no more than Chrétien meant,
because he worked with the consent
of Chrétien, who wrote the start.
He took the tale up at the part
where Lancelot was walled up fast,
7110   and he stayed with it to the last.
He wrote so much, no more, no less,
lest it be spoiled by awkwardness.

NOTES

Introduction

1. See Jean Frappier, *Chrétien de Troyes* (Paris: Hatier, 1968) and the English translation entitled *Chrétien de Troyes: The Man and His Work*, trans. Raymond J. Cormier (Athens: Ohio University Press, 1982); Urban T. Holmes, Jr., *Chrétien de Troyes* (New York: Twayne Publishers, 1970); F. Douglas Kelly, *Sens and Conjointure in the "Chevalier de la Charrette"* (The Hague and Paris: Mouton and Company, 1966); and Roger Sherman Loomis, *Arthurian Tradition and Chrétien de Troyes* (New York: Columbia University Press, 1949) for comprehensive studies of Chrétien de Troyes' life and works.

2. See John F. Benton, "The Court of Champagne as a Literary Center," *Speculum* 36, no. 4 (October 1961): 551–591.

3. The French royal house of Capet was closely allied to the powerful house of Blois-Champagne at this time. Louis VII, who had taken Adele of Blois and Champagne as his third wife in 1160, married his two daughters by his first wife, Eleanor of Aquitaine, to Adele's older brothers. Marie was married to Henry, count of Champagne, and Alix was married to Theobald, count of Blois.

4. Chrétien introduces himself at the beginning of his second romance *Cligés* as:

> The one who wrote of *Erec and Enide*,
> translated the *Commandments of Ovid*,
> the *Art of Love* in French did write,
> and wrote about "The Shoulder Bite,"
> about King Mark and blonde Isolde,
> the metamorphosis retold
> of the "Hoopoe, Swallow, and Nightingale,"
> is now beginning a new tale.

(Chrétien de Troyes, *Cligés*, ed. Alexandre Micha [Paris: Champion, 1957], p. 1, my translation). *Erec and Enide* was the first Arthurian romance. The *Commandments of Ovid* were probably *Remedies for Love*. "The Shoulder Bite" was a version of the Pelops legend, in which Tantalus served up his son Pelops as a dish for the gods. The gods restored Pelops to life but had to replace his bitten shoulder with an ivory one. "Philomena" is a tale of Tereus, Procne, and Philomena, who were changed into a hoopoe, swallow, and nightingale as a punishment for their crimes. Gaston Paris found a transcription of "Philomena" by a Chrétien in a late thirteenth or early fourteenth century manuscript of *Ovide Moralisé* in 1884. Chrétien's songs are entitled "Amors tançon et bataille" and "D'amors qui m'a tolu a moi." See Frappier, *Chrétien de Troyes: The Man and His Work*, pp. 5–6 and 49–54.

5. L. T. Topsfield, in *Chrétien de Troyes: A Study of the Arthurian Romances* (Cambridge and New York: Cambridge University Press, 1981), pp. 13–14, states: "There is evidence that tales from this Celtic tradition were transmitted orally and were popular in France from about 1100, or even earlier. William of Malmesbury, in his *Historia Regum Anglorum* of 1125, declares that trifles of the Bretons, *nugae Bretonum*, were current in his day about Arthur, 'a man worthy not to be dreamed about in false fables but to be proclaimed in truthful works of literature.' In 1155, Wace also speaks of the many tales which the Bretons tell about the Round Table."

6. Greimas cites Godefroi, *Dictionnaire de l'Ancien Français* (Larousse), who traces the meaning of *roman* as "in the vernacular" as opposed to Latin, and Topsfield notes: "*Romanz*, used as a noun, can refer to speech in the vernacular, to a translation into the vernacular, or a vernacular literary work" (*Chrétien de Troyes*, p. 11). Previously the *romanz* form had been used for classical themes to tell of the Trojan War and the settlement of Britain, such as the *Roman de Thèbes*, *Roman d'Alexandre*, *Roman de Troie*, and *Roman d'Enéas*. Wace also used this form for his translation of Geoffrey of Monmouth's *History of the Kings of England* (the *Roman de Brut*).

7. The dates of Chrétien's romances are disputed, and the dates in the introduction are the widely accepted ones given by Frappier in *Chrétien de Troyes: The Man and His Work*, p. 6. William A. Nitze proposed the earliest range of dates (1158–1181), in *Perceval and the Holy Grail*, University of California Publications in Modern Philology, vol. 28, no. 5 (Berkeley and Los Angeles: University of California Press, 1949), pp. 284–285; and Claude A. Luttrell proposes a shorter range of dates between 1184 and 1190, in *The Creation of the First Arthurian Romance: A Quest* (London: Edward Arnold, 1974).

8. In connection with the Arthur of myth and legend, Geoffrey Ashe notes that Arthur has been interpreted as a wind-god, a bird-god, a leader of the Wild Hunt riding thunderclouds, the Gaulish Artaean Mercury, and a spirit of vegetation dying and reviving in fertility rites, in *King Arthur's Avalon: The Story of Glastonbury* (Glasgow: William Collins Sons and Co., Fontana Books, 1980), p. 81.

Moreover, it is troubling that the contemporary Gildas, who wrote *De Excidio Britannia* (*On the Ruin of Britain*) before 547, fails to mention Arthur.

The earliest accounts mention the victory at Mount Badon without naming the commander; Gildas claims that the siege of Mount Badon occurred in the year of his birth, approximately forty-four years earlier. The Venerable Bede, who wrote *The Ecclesiastical History of the English People* in 731, like Gildas, his source, mentions the Saxon invasion of Britain and Mount Badon but does not mention Arthur. See Aubrey E. Galyon, "Bede," in *The Arthurian Encyclopedia*, ed. Norris J. Lacy (New York and London: Garland Publishing, 1986) p. 42.

9. Arthur is referred to in history and fiction, although the distinction was less clear in those times, when historical works might include deliberately biased and fantastical accounts of allegedly historical events and poems might contain obvious kernels of historical truth.

10. Richard Barber, in *King Arthur, Hero and Legend* (Woodbridge, Suffolk: Boydell Press, 1986), p. 2.

11. The prevailing opinion, largely because of the Welsh sources, is that there is more to Arthur than myth. Thomas Jones, "The Early Evolution of the Legend of Arthur," *Nottingham Medieval Studies* 8 (1964): 4, notes the lack of contemporary references to Arthur but states: "I accept the idea that there was a historical person of the name of Arthur early in the sixth century, who may have been one of the leaders of the Britons against their enemies, whoever they were, the Picts or Scots or Saxons, or any combination thereof."

The earliest reference to Arthur is in a Welsh poem the *Gododdin*, dated A.D. 600, which mentions that a particular hero fought bravely, "though he was no Arthur." Jones writes: "Whatever its date, the reference confirms the historicity of Arthur, because there are no references in early Welsh heroic poetry to legendary or unhistorical figures" (p. 13).

In A.D. 955 the *Annales Cambriae* (*The Annals of Wales*), whose other entries include references to real people, contain two entries for the following years:

518 The battle of Badon, in which Arthur carried the cross of Our Lord Jesus Christ for three days and three nights on his shoulders, and the Britons were the victors.

539 The battle of Camlaun, in which Arthur and Medraut were slain; and there was death in England and Ireland. (Ashe, p. 75).

Barber, while questioning the dates, believes that the events recorded in the *Annals* were part of the current historical tradition (*King Arthur, Hero and Legend*, pp. 6–7).

Other Welsh poems circulated long before Chrétien's era, although they were not written down until the thirteenth century. "The Stanzas of the

Graves" in the *Black Book of Carmarthen* says that the grave of Arthur is an eternal wonder and no one knows where it is. In the tale of Culhwch and Olwen in the same book Arthur lists his companions, including Kay and Bedivere. The poem "The Spoils of Annwfn" in the *Book of Taliesin* describes Arthur's raiding the Otherworld for its treasure (Patrick Ford, "Celtic Arthurian Literature," in *Arthurian Encyclopedia*, p. 91).

The Welsh *Historia Brittonum* (*The History of the Britons*), compiled around A.D. 800 to serve the interests of the contemporary Welsh people and whose authorship is attributed to Nennius, contains the reference: "Arthur fought against the Saxons alongside the kings of the Britons, but he himself was a leader in the battles (dux bellorum)." The "Nennius" history lists Arthur's twelve battles with the Saxons, most notably the eighth "by Castle Guinnion, in which Arthur carried on his shoulders an image of St. Mary Ever-Virgin, and on that day the pagans were put to flight" and the twelfth "on Mount Badon, in which—on that one day—there fell in one onslaught of Arthur's 960 men, and none slew them but he alone, and in all his battles he remained victor" (Ashe, *King Arthur's Avalon*, p. 73).

Barber notes that the "Nennius" history contains an account of the marvels of Britain, including a stone with the footprint of Arthur's dog Cafall, which mysteriously appears at the top of a cairn when removed, and the tomb of Arthur's son Amr, which is never the same size (p. 5).

See David N. Dumville, " 'Nennius' and the '*Historia Brittonum*,' " *Studia Celtae* 10–11 (1975–1976): 78–95; and F. Liebermann, "Nennius: The Author of the *Historia Brittonum*," in *Essays in Medieval History presented to T. F. Font*, ed. A. G. Little and F. M. Pewicke (Manchester: Manchester University Press, 1925), pp. 25–44.

12. Ashe notes, "From Land's End to the Grampian foothills, Arthur's name 'cleaves to cairn and cromlech.' We hear of the Cornish fortress at Kelliwic; of a Cornish hill called Bann Arthur and a stream called the River of Arthur's Kitchen; of Cadbury and its noble shades; of the lake Llyn Berfog in Merioneth where Arthur slew a monster, and his horse left a hoof-print on the rock; of a cave by Marchlyn Mawr in Caernarvon, where his treasure lies hidden (woe to any intruder who touches it); of a cave at Caerleon, and another near Snowdon, where his warriors lie asleep till he needs them; of still another cave in the Eildon hills, close to Melrose Abbey, where some say he is sleeping himself; of the mount outside Edinburgh called Arthur's Seat; of Arthur's Stone, and Arthur's Fold, as far north as Perth; and many more such places. Arthur seems to be everywhere" (Ashe, *King Arthur's Avalon*, pp. 98–99).

Geoffrey Ashe notes in "Camelot" (*Arthurian Encyclopedia*, p. 75) that Malory identifies Camelot with Winchester and in "Cadbury-Camelot" (p. 72) that Cadbury Castle in Somerset has long been designated by the name Camelot. Barber counters that Cadbury is: "a fascinating site, but one whose association with Arthur is so far pure wishful thinking" (*King Arthur, Hero and Legend*, p. 7).

Not Camelot, but Caerleon-on-Usk, in southeast Wales, is the city that Geoffrey of Monmouth associates with Arthur:

> When the feast of Whitsuntide began to draw near, Arthur, who was quite overjoyed by his great success, made up his mind to hold a plenary court at that season and to place the crown of the kingdom on his head. He decided, too, to summon to this feast the leaders who owed him homage, so that he could celebrate Whitsun with greater reverence and renew the closest possible pacts of peace with his chieftains. He explained to the members of his court what he was proposing to do and accepted their advice that he should carry out his plan in the City of the Legions.
>
> Situated as it is in Glamorganshire, on the River Usk, not far from the Severn Sea, in a most pleasant position, and being richer in material wealth than other townships, this city was eminently suitable for such a ceremony. The river which I have named flowed by it on one side, and up this the kings and princes who were to come from across the sea could be carried in a fleet of ships. On the other side, which was flanked by meadows and wooded groves, they had adorned the city with royal palaces, and by the gold-painted gables of its roofs it was a match for Rome. What is more, it was famous for its two churches. One of these, built in honour of the martyr Julius, was served by a monastery of canons, and counted as the third metropolitan see of Britain. The city also contained a college of two hundred learned men, who were skilled in astronomy and the other arts, and who watched with great attention the courses of the stars and so by their careful computations prophesied for King Arthur any prodigies due at that time.
>
> It was this city, therefore, famous for such a wealth of pleasant things, which was made ready for the feast. (Geoffrey of Monmouth, *The History of the Kings of Britain*, trans. Lewis Thorpe [1966; reprint, Harmondsworth, Middlesex: Penguin Books, 1979], bk. 9, ch. 12, pp. 225–227).

Geoffrey of Monmouth's description of Caerleon as the seat of Arthur's court is probably more valuable as literature than history; Barber notes that the only city this luxurious even in twelfth-century Europe was Constantinople, "clearly one model for Geoffrey's City of Legions" (*King Arthur, Hero and Legend*, p. 36). It should be noted that this beautiful city where Arthur holds his plenary court at Pentecost is a Roman city, not a fourteenth-century castle with turrets. Geoffrey Ashe, "Caerleon" (*Arthurian Encyclopedia*, pp. 74–75), notes that a large number of the Roman buildings in Caerleon have been excavated and the amphitheater is the finest specimen in Britain.

13. See Geoffrey Ashe, "Arthur, Origin of Legend" (*Arthurian Encyclopedia*, p. 23), for a discussion of the theory advanced by R. G. Collingwood, in R. G. Collingwood and J. N. L. Myres, *Roman Britain and the English Settlements* (London and New York: Oxford University Press, 1937), that this leader was Roman-trained and a master of light cavalry, so that, when a town was threatened by an invasion of Saxons, a company of mounted knights would strike suddenly in its defense and then move elsewhere they were needed. Barber skeptically refers to this theory as part of "the archaeological myth of Arthur" (*King Arthur, Hero and Legend*, p. 7).

14. The date given for the Battle of Camlann in the *Annales Cambriae* is 539. Geoffrey of Monmouth gives 542.

15. Yet these historical accounts contain the seeds for the subsequent well-developed episodes of the literary King Arthur. A fellowship transcending rank could have developed among his company of knights, which would later be symbolized by the Round Table, where because of its shape none of Arthur's knights took precedence. Any marital problems suffered by an often-absent leader married to one of the most desirable women of the land may be reflected in the tales of Guinevere and her infidelity. The tale of Mordred's treachery and betrayal may express the plots and intrigues that surround the powerful. And, understandably, when so feared a leader fell in battle, his followers might have attempted to conceal his death from his foes, giving rise to the legend that Arthur was not dead but sleeping and would come again to Britain in her hour of need.

In contrast to this legend, modern tourists to Glastonbury visit what is supposedly the site of Arthur's grave. Henry II learned the rumor that Arthur's grave was located between two pillars in Glastonbury Abbey at an earlier date, but no excavations were made until the Abbey suffered a fire in 1184, the church burned, and subsequently fundraising became important. In 1190 excavations were begun; seven feet down the diggers conveniently found a stone slab and a cross bearing the inscription, "Here lies buried the renowned King Arthur in the Isle of Avalon." At sixteen feet the diggers found a hollowed oaken log containing the bones of an exceptionally tall, sixth-century warrior slain by a crushing blow to the skull and the bones of a small blonde woman. The prevailing opinion is that the cross was "an able forgery" but the coffin seemed genuinely to date from the sixth century (Ashe, *King Arthur's Avalon*, pp. 179–183).

16. Three of Chrétien's works have parallels with Welsh romances that

circulated orally for many years and were written down in the thirteenth century in the *Mabinogi: Geraint and Enid* (*Erec and Enide*), *Owain and the Lady of the Fountain* (*Yvain*), and *Peredur, Son of Efrog* (*Perceval*). Their relationship to Chrétien's works is unclear; it is not known whether they are adaptations of his romances or share a common remote source with them (see Brynley F. Roberts, in *Arthurian Encyclopedia*, p. 412).

17. In 1125 William of Malmesbury, in his *Acts of the Kings of England*, refers to "the distinguished achievement of the warlike Arthur . . . of whom the trifling of the Britons tells so much nonsense even today, a man clearly worthy not to be dreamed of in fallacious fable, but to be proclaimed in veracious histories, as one who long sustained his tottering country." William also describes Arthur's rout of nine hundred enemy at the siege of Badon, bearing the image of the Virgin (Ashe, *King Arthur's Avalon*, p. 75).

In 1130 Caradoc of Llancarfan, in the *Life of St. Gildas*, describes Melwas's abduction of Guinevere to Glastonbury and Arthur's rescue of her.

18. References to the last battle appear in Geoffrey Monmouth's *The History of the Kings of Britain:*

> When summer came, Arthur made ready to set out for Rome, and was already beginning to make his way through the mountains when the news was brought to him that his nephew Mordred, in whose care he had left Britain, had placed the crown upon his own head. What is more, this treacherous tyrant was living adulterously and out of wedlock with Queen Guinevere, who had broken the vows of her earlier marriage. . . . Surrounded by this enormous army, in which he placed his hope, Mordred marched to meet Arthur as soon as the latter landed at Richborough. In the battle which ensued Mordred inflicted great slaughter on those who were trying to land . . . Gawain, the King's nephew, died that day, together with many others too numerous to describe. In the end, but only with enormous difficulty, Arthur's men occupied the seashore. They drove Mordred and his army before them in flight and inflicted great slaughter on them in their turn. . . . When this was announced to Queen Guinevere, she gave way to despair. She fled from York to the City of the Legions, and there, in the church of Julius the Martyr, she took her vows among the nuns, promising to lead a chaste life. . . . The accursed traitor was killed . . . Arthur himself, our renowned King, was mortally wounded and was carried off to the Isle of Avalon, so that his wounds might be attended to. He handed the crown of Britain over to his cousin Constantine, the son of Cador Duke of Cornwall: this in the year 542 after our Lord's Incarnation. (10: 257–261).

For analyses of the inaccuracies and biases in Geoffrey of Monmouth's work, see Barber, *King Arthur, Hero and Legend*, pp. 24–37; Christopher

Brooke, "Geoffrey of Monmouth as a Historian," in *Church and Government in the Middle Ages,* ed. C. Brooke et al. (Cambridge: Cambridge University Press, 1976), pp. 77–91; and Valerie I. J. Flint, "The *Historia Regum Britanniae* of Geoffrey of Monmouth: Parody and Its Purpose, a Suggestion," *Speculum* 54 (July 1979): 447–468.

19. Wace, who dedicated his *Roman de Brut* to Eleanor of Aquitaine, was the first to mention the Round Table and the Breton Hope of Arthur's return. See William W. Kibler, "Wace," in *Arthurian Encyclopedia,* pp. 615–616. See Topsfield, *Chrétien de Troyes,* pp. 6–7; and Tom Peete Cross and William A. Nitze, *Lancelot and Guinevere: A Study on the Origins of Courtly Love* (Chicago: University of Chicago Press, 1930), pp. 20–21. See the Introduction to *La Portée Arturienne du Roman de Brut,* ed. I. D. O. Arnold and M. M. Pelan (Paris: Klincksieck, 1962).

20. Cross and Nitze observe that Lancelot's hospitable hosts and perilous passages (the Water Bridge, Sword Bridge, and falling portcullis) are in the tradition of Celtic visits to the Otherworld (*Lancelot and Guinevere,* pp. 53–54).

21. Cross and Nitze note that the *Book of Leinster* circa 1150 lists twelve stories called *aitheda* or elopements (*Lancelot and Guinevere,* pp. 32–33).

22. According to Cross and Nitze the following motifs of such Celtic tales are present in *Lancelot:* The wife is abducted by a "marvellous" being who lives in a supernatural realm with barriers. She is either kidnapped suddenly or won in combat or through a 'rash boon' (see note to v. 157) from her husband, but her abductor does not possess her sexually at once. The abductor is pursued by her husband, possibly with an escort, or her husband's man who is her lover (*Lancelot and Guinevere,* pp. 20, 31–32).

23. Cross and Nitze mention the precedent of the old Celtic tale *Tochmarc Etaine.* Etain, a fairy and the wife of a fairy prince, was reborn a mortal and married King Eochaid of Ireland. Her Otherworld husband finally reclaimed her and carried her home (*Lancelot and Guinevere,* pp. 57–59).

24. See Topsfield, *Chrétien de Troyes,* p. 108; and Geoffrey Ashe, "Gildas," in *Arthurian Encyclopedia,* p. 235.

25. See William W. Kibler, "Lancelot," in *Arthurian Encyclopedia,* p. 324.

26. Norris J. Lacy, "Béroul," in *Arthurian Encyclopedia,* p. 45; and William W. Kibler, "Thomas d'Angleterre," in *Arthurian Encyclopedia,* pp. 549–550.

27. Eleanor of Aquitaine, daughter of William X, duke of Aquitaine and count of Poitiers, a great heiress whose beauty was celebrated by the troubadours, became queen of France at the age of fifteen upon her marriage to Louis VII in 1137. After the birth of two daughters, Marie and Alix, her marriage to Louis VII was annulled, and Eleanor married Henry, count of Anjou, the great-grandson of William the Conqueror, in 1152 and became

queen of England upon his accession as Henry II in 1154. After the birth of eight children, including five sons (William, who died in childhood; Henry, the Young King; Richard the Lion-Heart; Geoffrey, duke of Brittany; and John Lackland), Eleanor separated from Henry II, who was involved in his famous love affair with Rosamond Clifford, and reestablished her court at Poitiers in 1167. Her daughter, Countess Marie, may have visited her around 1170. Eleanor lived in Poitiers until she supported her sons in their conspiracy against Henry II and was arrested in 1174. After sixteen years of imprisonment, her fortunes were restored when Henry II died in 1189. Under the reign of her son Richard, she proved an able administrator of his realm, especially during his crusade, and she was an asset to her son King John until she died in 1204. See Marion Meade, *Eleanor of Aquitaine: A Biography* (New York: Hawthorn/Dutton, 1977), for a biography of Eleanor of Aquitaine and pp. 67, 148, 249–251, 294, 322, 338, for references to Countess Marie.

The count and countess of Champagne had two sons: Henry II (1166), King of Jerusalem, and Thibaut (1179); and two daughters: Marie and Scholastique. Benton notes that after Henry of Champagne's death in 1181, the thirty-six-year-old widow Marie remained an excellent administrator for both sons in their minority until her death in 1198 ("Court of Champagne," p. 554). Meade describes Marie's conservative upbringing at the French court and observes: "More than any of Eleanor's children, including Richard, Marie was her mother's child . . . Marie was already a person of some consequence in her own right . . . Unlike the Capetian court, her new home at Troyes was a center of culture and taste in northern France, and its sophisticated court a gathering place for poets such as Chrétien de Troyes. Marie gives the impression of being an aggressive woman who carved spheres of influence for herself, but, less politically minded than Eleanor, she took for her province of expertise the literary . . . and became a patroness of the arts" (Meade, *Eleanor of Acquitaine*, p. 229).

28. See Benton, "Court of Champagne," for a detailed account of the writers who received support and encouragement from the count and countess of Champagne.

29. Foster E. Guyer, "The Influence of Ovid on Chrétien de Troyes," *Romanic Review* 12, no. 2–3 (1921): 218, describes the influence of Ovid's *Art of Love, Remedies for Love,* and *Metamorphoses* on Chrétien's works: "Many figures of speech in Crestien's poems are taken from those of the Roman poet. The long love monologues in Crestien's romances are modeled upon Ovid's and in some cases are composed of elements taken directly from the works of the teacher and doctor of love."

For the Arabic roots of courtly love, see Alois Richard Nykl, *Hispano-*

Arab Poetry and Its Relations with the Old Provençal Troubadours (Baltimore: J. H. Furst Company, 1946).

30. See William D. Paden, Jr., "The Troubadour's Lady: Her Marital Status and Social Rank," *Studies in Philology* 72 (1975): 28–50.

31. See Meg Bogin, *The Women Troubadours* (New York and London: W. W. Norton and Company, 1980), pp. 37–61, the chapter entitled "Courtly Love: A New Interpretation."

32. Topsfield, *Chrétien de Troyes*, pp. 4, 8–9.

33. Topsfield notes that in the lyric poetry of the troubadours the lover might be rewarded for his patience by a sleeve or ribbon, a kiss, or possibly a nude embrace. Physical consummation was a strongly desired but virtually unattainable goal (*Chrétien de Troyes*, p. 109). See Peter S. Noble, *Love and Marriage in Chrétien de Troyes* (Cardiff: University of Wales Press, 1982), pp. 1–11, for a discussion of these aspects of courtly love.

34. See Bogin, *Women Troubadours*, pp. 53–54. Meade notes that Eleanor's troubadour Bernart de Ventadorn "had been banished from his last place of employment for making improper advances to the lady of the castle" (*Eleanor of Aquitaine*, p. 159).

35. Andreas Capellanus wrote *The Art of Courtly Love* (*De Amore*) in 1185. He records and possibly parodies the "courts of love" and gives the "rules of love" with which Lancelot's reveries, fainting spells, and other exaggerated emotional reactions are perfectly consistent (see W. T. H. Jackson, "The *De Amore* of Andreas Capellanus and the Practice of Love at Court," *Romanic Review* 49 (1958): 243–251; Mildred Leake Day, "Andreas Capellanus," in *Arthurian Encyclopedia*, p. 7; and Norris J. Lacy, "Courtly Love," in *Arthurian Encyclopedia*, p. 122). In Andreas Capellanus, *The Art of Courtly Love*, trans. John Jay Parry and ed. Frederick W. Locke (New York: Frederick Ungar Publishing Co., 1957), Lady Ermengarde of Narbonne gives her decision in a love case: "We consider that marital affection and the true love of lovers are wholly different and arise from entirely different sources, and so the ambiguous nature of the word prevents the comparison of the things, and we have to place them in different classes" (p. 33). In another case, Queen Eleanor comments: "We dare not oppose the opinion of the Countess of Champagne, who ruled that love can exert no power between husband and wife" (p. 34). Certain of the rules of love that apply to *Lancelot* include:

I. Marriage is no real excuse for not loving.

V. That which a lover takes against the will of his beloved has no relish.

IX. No one can love unless he is impelled by the persuasion of love.

XII. A true lover does not desire to embrace in love anyone except his beloved.

XIV. The easy attainment of love makes it of little value; difficulty of attainment makes it prized.

XV. Every lover regularly turns pale in the presence of his beloved.

XVI. When a lover suddenly catches sight of his beloved his heart palpitates.

XXIII. He whom the thought of love vexes eats and sleeps very little.

XXV. A true lover considers nothing good except what he thinks will please his beloved.

XXVI. Love can deny nothing to love.

XXVII. A lover can never have enough of the solaces of his beloved.

XXX. A true lover is constantly and without intermission possessed by the thought of his beloved. (Andreas Capellanus, *Art of Courtly Love*, pp. 42–43)

Kelly covers the influence of Andreas Capellanus on *Lancelot* extensively in *Sens and Conjointure*, pp. 31–69.

36. In *Erec and Enide*, the young prince Erec falls in love with the impoverished noble maiden Enide and marries her; because of his passionate love for his bride he neglects his knightly obligations. Stung that Enide feels that he is a lesser man for marrying her, he sets off to prove his prowess to her by rescuing her from a series of foes. When he is reassured of her love and his prowess they are reconciled, and the romance ends with their coronation at Nantes. In *Cligés*, which is heavily indebted to the Tristan legend despite its Byzantine setting, Fenice, married against her will to King Alis, feigns death with a potion so that she can be reunited with his nephew Cligés, saying scornfully that she will not be like that slut Iseut, and he who has her heart shall have her body. In *Yvain*, Chrétien's best constructed romance, which was probably written concurrently with *Lancelot*, the knight Yvain marries the widowed Laudine after slaying her husband in fair combat at her fountain, and then he thoughtlessly forgets his promise to return to her after a year of separation. She rejects him utterly, and after a period of heartbreak and madness Yvain befriends a lion who becomes his companion and devotes himself to the service of women in need. Fighting incognito as the Knight with the Lion, he obtains a succession of victories in matches where he is either outnumbered or pitted against gigantic and supernatural foes until he returns to his lady a better man and obtains the forgiveness he now deserves.

There are three specific references to *Lancelot* in *Yvain* and numerous parallels in *Lancelot* to *Yvain*, so these two tales of courtly love inside and outside marriage are intertwined. David J. Shirt, in "How Much of the Lion Can We Put Before the Cart?" *French Studies* 31 (1977), concludes that Chrétien first wrote *Yvain* vv. 1–2000, then wrote *Lancelot* vv. 1–5358 concurrently with *Yvain* vv. 2001–4739. At that point he turned *Lancelot* over to Godefroy de Leigny while he finished *Yvain*. After Godefroy had finished *Lancelot*, Chrétien wrote vv. 5359–6131 containing the description of the tournament and the construction of the tower (with the minor inconsistency that Chrétien's tower is on an island in the inlet whereas Godefroy's tower is on the shore and accessible by land) and inserted this passage between the queen's return to court and Godefroy's conclusion.

37. Lancelot overtakes Meleagant, the queen, and their large party on the first day but is defeated in combat and delayed by walking until he comes upon the cart. Lancelot and Gawain catch sight of the queen and Meleagant's party on the second day but are unable to overtake the party. Lancelot discovers the queen's comb by the fountain on the third day, which indicates that she had passed that way recently and probably had used a captive's trick of discarding a personal object to keep her rescuers on her trail. She knew Lancelot was pursuing her as of his skirmish on the first day. Since Lancelot spends the third night in Gorre with the first captive vavasor, the queen may have passed into Gorre as early as the third day and, if Meleagant knew a direct way to Bademagu's fortress, have been Bademagu's guest for three days. Yet, when the queen leaves with a large party, King Bademagu and she do not cross the Water or Sword Bridge, and her party takes six days to rejoin Arthur's court. Applying conventional measurements of time and space to Otherworld literary realms is always a dubious endeavor.

38. Frappier, *Chrétien de Troyes: The Man and His Work*, p. 102. The tales of Euridice and Persephone are contained in Ovid's *Metamorphoses*; Euripides dramatized the tale of Alcestis and Admetus.

39. See Matilda Tomaryn Bruckner, "*Le Chevalier de la Charrette* (*Lancelot*)," in *The Romances of Chrétien de Troyes: A Symposium*, ed. Douglas Kelly (Lexington, Ky.: French Forum Publishers, 1985), p. 155, who in turn refers to Jacques Ribard's interpretation of the entire romance as Christian allegory, in *Chrétien de Troyes, Le Chevalier de la Charrette: Essai d'interprétation symbolique* (Paris: Nizet, 1972).

40. Chrétien is not overly severe and may have found the possibility of inconstancy worse than adultery, for he presents Lancelot and Guinevere as motivated by deep and sincere mutual love. An interesting intertextual inconsistency is that the last reference to *Lancelot* in *Yvain* refers to Lancelot's captivity in the tower immediately after the queen's return from Gorre, when the younger daughter of the Lord of the Black Thorn arrives at court

> three days past the day
> that Arthur's queen returned home free
> from Meleagant's captivity.
> By treachery and evil power

Sir Lancelot was in the tower
a captive.

(Chrétien de Troyes, *Yvain, or The Knight with the Lion,* trans. Ruth Harwood Cline [Athens: University of Georgia Press, 1975], p. 134), whereas in *Lancelot* the hero spends some time under house arrest and attends the great tournament at Worstede. After a careful analysis of Chrétien's choice of rhyme over *Erec, Cligés, Lancelot,* and *Yvain,* which shows a steady decline in the use of assonance and consonance and increased use of perfect rhymes of one, two, or more syllables, Shirt postulates in "How Much of the Lion Can We Put Before the Cart?" that Chrétien inserted the tournament at Worstede episode because he had read with dissatisfaction Godefroy de Leigny's conclusion, in which Lancelot seems to have forgotten Guinevere and the importance of the last battle to determine her fate, and his stay with Meleagant's sister is given prominence. The tournament episode, which firmly establishes that the lovers are totally one another's, shows that their love is even deeper than it was during their night together in Gorre and places Lancelot's understandable affection for his young rescuer in its proper perspective.

41. For excellent studies of these love relationships, see Kelly, *Sens and Conjointure;* Bruckner, *"Le Chevalier de la Charrette"* and "An Interpreter's Dilemma: Why Are There So Many Interpretations of Chrétien's *Chevalier de la Charrette?" Romance Philology* 40 (1986–1987): 159–180, and Topsfield, *Chrétien de Troyes.*

42. *Perceval,* vv. 8174–8199, may be taken as Chrétien's final opinion of the queen, when Sir Gawain describes her to Queen Ygerne:

My lady, there's no disagreeing:
she is so very beautiful,
so very courteous, so full
of wisdom, that God in His grace
has not created any place
of other law or language where
one could find anyone so fair.
No lady's been so glorified
since the Lord God took Adam's side
and the first woman was thus raised,
and she deserves to be so praised.
As the schoolmaster, wise and keen,
instructs small children, so the queen
instructs us, and is always giving

the world a model of good living.
From her all virtues radiate,
and spring forth, and originate,
and everyone at court who grieves
is comforted before he leaves.
Our gracious queen has always guessed
each person's true worth and how best
to please him, and has done or said it.
The man with fine deeds to his credit
has learned them from the things she taught.
No man, however overwrought,
has left my lady angrily.

(Chrétien de Troyes, *Perceval; or, The Story of the Grail*, trans. Ruth Harwood Cline [Athens: University of Georgia Press, 1985], pp. 217–218).

43. Some scholars consider Gawain's manner cool and others not; knights of the Round Table addressed one another formally. Gawain undoubtedly recognized Lancelot by his arms (there is no indication that Lancelot, like Yvain, took time to disguise himself on his quest) and certainly when they removed their helmets at dinner that first evening. If such coolness exists, Chrétien's version heralds later versions of the romance, when Gawain, the king's nephew, becomes Lancelot's enemy when his brothers discover the love affair and are killed.

44. Kelly observes in *Sens and Conjointure*, p. 217: "It is by the union of Guenevere's very real passion with the conventional traits of the courtly lady that Chrétien succeeded in creating a woman capable of fascinating men's minds down to the end of the Middle Ages, a Guenevere devoid of both the coldly distant impersonality of the lady of lyric poetry and of the ferociously possessive sensuality which characterizes her in Marie de France's 'Lanval.'"

45. For the character of Lancelot in the prose continuations, see William W. Kibler, "Lancelot," in *Arthurian Encyclopedia*, p. 325; and E. Jane Burns, "Vulgate Cycle," in *Arthurian Encyclopedia*, pp. 610ff.

46. Dhira B. Mahoney, "Stanzaic *Le Morte Arthur*," in *Arthurian Encyclopedia*, pp. 525–526.

47. William W. Kibler, "Lancelot," in *Arthurian Encyclopedia*, p. 325.

48. Kelly, *Sens et Conjointure*, p. 27.

49. Chrétien de Troyes, *Le Chevalier de la Charrete*, ed. Mario Roques (Paris: Champion, 1970). Albert Foulet, "Appendix I: On Editing Chrétien's Lancelot," in *The Romances of Chrétien de Troyes: A Symposium*, pp. 287–309.

50. Chrétien differentiated among the present, future, imperfect, and past

tenses more consistently than many of his contemporaries, as Tatania Fotitch noted in her study *The Narrative Tenses in Chrétien de Troyes* (Washington, D.C.: Catholic University of America Press, 1950). Nonetheless, Chrétien shifts from the past to the historical present tense, sometimes to give immediacy to a passage and sometimes for no evident reason, a feature of Old French discussed more fully by William W. Kibler, *An Introduction to Old French* (New York: Modern Language Association of America, 1984), pp. 93–94. In twentieth-century English immediacy is conveyed more effectively by choice of vocabulary than by a tense shift, and continuous switching from past to present tense can be irritating. In some much-analyzed vocabulary in *Lancelot,* the Old French *san* means sense, good sense, meaning, and direction; *antancion* means both careful attention and purpose or intention, in the dual sense of the adjective "intent"; and *droit chemin* means both the straight way and the right way.

51. See Kibler, *Introduction to Old French,* pp. xxiii–xxvii, for a comprehensive review of Old French dialects and the "twelfth-century renaissance" in the language.

52. Kibler, *Introduction to Old French,* pp. 2–4.

53. Adjectives like *bel* (dear, good, handsome, beautiful, kind), *gent* (noble, courteous, nice, handsome), *sage* (wise, prudent, well-behaved), *fel* (treacherous, cruel, violent), and *vil* (vile, disgraceful, low-born) are used constantly and must be translated in context with variety.

54. Some key phrases that are repeated in *Lancelot* are the numerous references to "the straight/right way" and "better or worse," King Bademagu's admonition to Meleagant "I warn and urge you to make peace" (vv. 3236 and 3247), the queen's decision to halt the duel "I would have Lancelot hold back" (vv. 3794 and 3807–3808), the herald's cry at the tournament "the one has come to take their measure" (vv. 5563–5564, 5571, 5617–5618, 5682, and 5964) and the idea that Lancelot "pardons once but never twice" (vv. 904, 2860, 4984).

55. Prose translations of *Lancelot* are available for persons who are interested in Chrétien solely as a storyteller. Among others, Jean Frappier prepared a modern French translation, and D. D. R. Owen has prepared a modern English translation. William W. Kibler has prepared the equivalent of an interlinear English translation with the Old French and English texts on facing pages. All are valuable contributions to the study of Chrétien de Troyes.

56. Shirt, "How Much of the Lion Can We Put Before the Cart?" p. 9.

57. See Foulet, "Appendix I"; Shirt, "How Much of the Lion Can We Put Before the Cart?" and "Godefroy de Lagny et la composition de la *Char-*

rette," *Romania* 96 (1975): 27–52; and Frappier, *Chrétien de Troyes: The Man and His Work,* p. 179, for analyses of the characteristics of Chrétien's verse. In *Lancelot,* in addition to simpler rhymes like *va/trova, ot/plot/sot,* Chrétien uses noun-verb homonyms like *avoir/avoir* (vv. 1483–1484, Roques edition), *qui porte/une porte* (vv. 5799–5800), and pairs *Logres/ogres* (vv. 3517–3518) in the analogy of the people of *Logres* gathering as people do to hear the *organs* at the festivals, *Londres/arondres* (vv. 5817–5818) in the description of the *London*-made shield bearing two *swallows.* Godefroy de Leigny pairs *Gant/ Meleagant* (vv. 6719–6720) to say that not for all the riches between Babylon and *Ghent* would Lancelot let *Meleagant* escape.

58. Patricia Terry, my professor of literary translation, used iambic tetrameter to render *octosyllabe* in her translations of *Lays of Courtly Love* (New York: Doubleday and Company, Anchor Books, 1963).

Text

1. Countess Marie of Champagne was the daughter of Louis VII and Eleanor of Aquitaine and the wife of Count Henry of Champagne.

12–13. The interpretation of these verses is disputed, and this translation is based on the new interpretation of the passage by Karl Uitti, in "Autant en Emporte Li Funs: Remarques sur le Prologue du *Chevalier de la Charrette* de Chrétien de Troyes," *Romania* 105 (1984): 270–291. Manuscript C reads:

> . . . *qui sont vivanz*
> *si con li funs passe les vanz*
> *qui vante en mai ou en avril.*

[The countess surpasses all living (*vivanz*) ladies as *li funs* (singular subject) surpasses the winds (*les vanz,* rhymes with *vivanz,* plural object) that blows (singular verb) in May or in April.] Foerster speculated that *li funs* might be the foehn, a warm dry west wind that blows down the side of the Swiss Alps with considerable force, so that the translation would be "as the foehn which blows in May or in April surpasses the winds." The foehn is a violent and nerve-wracking wind, so that such a comparison is not a particularly flattering one, and Uitti notes that *funs* is used in other medieval texts and in Chrétien's works with the meaning of the modern French *fumée:* smoke, vapor given off by the land, or misty breath on a cold day. In *Cligés,* v. 596, Chrétien pairs "*flame ne funs*" with the clear meaning of flame and smoke. Gaston Paris suggested that the subject of the phrase should be wind and the object *funs,* "*le fun passe li vanz,*" and the rich rhyme of *vivanz/li vanz* (subject form) supports this contention. Thus the translation would read "as the wind that blows in April or May surpasses smoke/mist." Uitti contends that this interpretation is supported by the Garrett 125 manuscript, to which Foerster and Paris did not have access, and which reads: ". . . *tant com le fu passe li vens / qui en mai vent u en avril.*" Uitti suggests that in a future edition *funs* could be plural and recommends that it be translated in the sense of the modern French *brumes*, fog and mist, and that *vanz* be translated as *breeze*, a word that did not exist in Old French. Thus the countess is likened to the gentle spring breezes that are welcomed after the fog and mist of winter.

19. Two queens with which the countess might have been compared in 1177 were her mother, Eleanor of Aquitaine, Queen of England; and her sister-in-law, Adele of Champagne, Queen of France.

30. Ascension Day falls forty days after Easter and ten days before the feast of Pentecost. Philippe Ménard, in "Note sur la date du Chevalier de la Charrette," *Romania* 92 (1974): 118–126, notes that the chronology of *Lancelot* and *Yvain* is fairly consistent with the exceptionally late Easter (April 24) that occurred in 1177. In that year Ascension Day fell on June 2 and Pentecost on June 12. In *Yvain* Pentecost falls, not in May as usual, but in June two weeks before the Feast of Saint John on June 24. In *Lancelot*, the hero crosses a mown meadow (v. 1835) (haying was always done in June) two days after Ascension Day. While this chronology is not evidence that Chrétien composed *Yvain* and *Lancelot* in 1177, it is likely that he had the late feasts of that year in mind.

30a. Caerleon. Geoffrey Ashe defines Caerleon as "a small town by the River Gwent, at the southeast corner of Wales" ("Caerleon," in *The Arthurian Encyclopedia*, ed. Norris J. Lacy [New York and London: Garland Publishing, 1986], pp. 74–75). Geoffrey of Monmouth mentions Caerleon as the site of Arthur's plenary court after his first Gallic campaign.

33a. Camelot. This is the earliest reference to King Arthur's court at Camelot in literature, and it is not present in MS C. Its location is unknown: Malory situates Camelot at Winchester, and recent excavations link it to Cadbury Castle in Somerset. Geoffrey Ashe describes this Iron-Age hill fort associated with the name Camelot that was reoccupied and refortified during the historic Arthur's day, with a unique stone and timber wall, sixteen feet thick, running three-quarters of a mile around the perimeter (see "Cadbury-Camelot" in *Arthurian Encyclopedia*, pp. 72–74). Norris J. Lacy notes that the importance of Camelot as a literary place far transcends its geographical location, observing "in the Arthurian Romance it is less a specific place than a state of mind, a source of inspiration, an idea" ("Camelot" in *Arthurian Encyclopedia*, pp. 75–76). .

30a and 33a. The verses referring to Caerleon and Camelot are not contained in MS C but are contained in MSS A, E, T, and Garrett 125. See Alfred Foulet, "Appendix I: On Editing Chrétien's Lancelot," in *The Romances of Chrétien de Troyes: A Symposium,* ed. Douglas Kelly (Lexington, Ky.: French Forum Publishers, 1985), p. 289.

40. The ladies conversing in French at the English court reflect the Norman conquest in 1066. The languages spoken by the historical Arthur's entourage would have been Celtic, Old English, or possibly Latin. After 1066, when Duke William of Normandy asserted his claim to the English throne by slaying Harold of Wessex, the Saxon successor to Edward the Confessor, the ruling class in England spoke French.

41. Kay, Arthur's foster brother and seneschal, or steward, while presented in the English versions of the Arthurian literature as a brave and worthy knight, is consistently portrayed by Chrétien as a boor and braggart and a poor fighter.

44. This unknown knight is the villain Meleagant, the son of King Bademagu of Gorre. The capital of Gorre is Bath, which seems to be located six days of hard riding from Caerleon, in Arthur's kingdom of Logres.

61. King Arthur is portrayed as exceedingly helpless in *Lancelot,* perhaps to make the queen's adultery more understandable. See David J. Shirt, "*Le Chevalier de la Charrette:* A World Upside Down?" *Modern Language Review* 76 (1981), for a discussion of Chrétien's use of this topos in *Lancelot* and *Cligés.* Meleagant's failure to greet the king, the king's meek acceptance of his insolence, the steward's resignation, and the queen's prostration at his feet are all reversals of the normal medieval hierarchy.

155–157. The rash boon motif, in which an individual promises to do something unknown, is a frequent impetus to the action in an Arthurian romance. Both the king and queen have committed themselves unwittingly. Chrétien's King Arthur is generous, seeks to please, and never goes back on his word, so he is quite vulnerable to this ploy. See Jean Frappier, "Le motif du don contraignant dans la littérature du moyen âge," *Travaux de linguistique et de littérature* 7 (1969): 7–46, reprinted in *Amour Courtois et Table Ronde* (Geneva: Droz, 1973), pp. 225–264.

209. MS C gives "Oh, king," MS A "Oh, friend," and MS T gives "Oh, Oh." "Oh, king" makes little sense; if the queen's lament is addressed to the king, even if she is suggesting that he did not realize the implications of the rash boon, there is no reason for her to say it softly so that no one would hear it, when the whole court is lamenting in a similar vein, and there is no significance to her being overheard by Count Guinables. It is far more likely that her lament is addressed to an absent friend or sweetheart, who did not know about Kay's escorting her and who was sufficiently concerned about

her not to have permitted it. The double meaning of the English "Oh, dear" captures the meaning of MSS A and T.

271. This knight is Lancelot. No explanation is given for his absence from the court on the Ascension Day feast or the manner in which the news of the queen's danger reached him, but he was at the distance required to ride a horse to death. There is no indication that he took time to change arms and disguise himself, so Sir Gawain knows his identity.

311. Meleagant came accompanied by more companions than Lancelot was able to overwhelm when he overtook Meleagant's party on the road to Gorre.

321ff. David J. Shirt notes that Chrétien has invented this cart of infamy as a combination of the French tumbril and the English "scolding cart" ("Chrétien de Troyes et une coutume anglaise," Romania 94 (1973): 178–195). The tumbril was used in France to transport criminals convicted of major crimes to the place of execution and was an object of horror, whereas the "scolding cart" was used in England like a pillory, to immobilize persons who had committed minor offenses and expose them to public ridicule and perhaps a ducking. Lancelot's cart inspires both dread and derision; he sits in it immobile, whether he is constrained physically or powerless otherwise to obtain information about the queen. By mounting the cart, he forfeits his property and the feudal honors to which his rank entitles him. Since he is traditionally a son of King Ban and as jealous of his reputation as Meleagant, the sacrifice is a great one.

330. Legal combat was based on the belief that God would give victory to the champion of the person who was in the right. It was undertaken after oaths were exchanged, so the loser was considered to be both wrong and forsworn and was punished accordingly.

348. Malevolent dwarves are often found in medieval literature, which tended to equate physical and moral qualities. A second dwarf appears in line 5058 and is equally harmful to Lancelot. In Yvain, a dwarf accompanies the giant Harpin of the Mountain and flogs his captives, who are Sir Gawain's nephews (Chrétien de Troyes, Yvain; or, The Knight with the Lion, trans. Ruth Harwood Cline [Athens: University of Georgia Press, 1975], vv. 3889ff, p. 115).

360a, b. MS C omits this line about the two steps Lancelot hesitates. Since the queen refers to these two steps in vv. 4484–4490, the omission is generally considered to be an oversight, although David F. Hult contends that MS C makes sense without the elaboration on the steps of delay at that point, in "Lancelot's Two Steps: A Problem in Textual Criticism," Speculum 61 (1986): 836–858.

365ff. Foster E. Guyer notes that Chrétien has emulated Ovid's personification of Love as a god who gives commands ("The Influence of Ovid on Chrétien de Troyes," *Romanic Review* 12, no. 2–3 [1921]: 227). See also vv. 1233ff.

514ff. L. T. Topsfield notes that in Celtic tradition the Flaming Lance, like the Perilous Bed, can only be dealt with by a great hero who is fit for the quest he has undertaken (*Chrétien de Troyes: A Study of the Arthurian Romances* [Cambridge and New York: Cambridge University Press, 1981], pp. 118–119). In this incident Lancelot counters the maiden's jeering and affirms his worth.

600. It seems supernatural that two knights, riding unencumbered and fast, one of them vowed to take the most direct way, are unable to overtake a party of knights and maidens transporting the queen on her palfrey and the injured Kay on his litter.

607. Topsfield notes that this maiden is a traditional guide to the Otherworld and by her allusion to the right or straight way reflects the troubadour Marcabru's reference to the right path to Love and the connotation of moral strength, which he contrasts with the wrong or crooked way (*Chrétien de Troyes*, p. 120). There are many Biblical precedents for the straight way, including Isaiah 40:3, "make straight in the desert a highway for our God," quoted by Luke 3:4 "and the crooked shall be made straight," and Jeremiah 31:9 "I will make them walk . . . in a straight path." This maiden never claims her promises, but she gives Chrétien an opportunity to show the effect of love on Lancelot, who is willing to promise anything and believes that there is nothing he cannot do.

640ff. This description of the kingdom of Gorre as the land of prisoners from which no strangers may return links it to the Celtic Otherworld and the classical Hades, both realms of the dead. Chrétien does not explain why good King Bademagu has been taking prisoners from Logres or why King Arthur has been unable to remedy the situation. Lancelot is hailed as the liberator of the captives, but their plight had been tolerated for years, and it was not until the queen was abducted that he or anyone else at court was motivated to take action.

669–673. Roger Sherman Loomis links the precedents for the Sword Bridge to Irish tales reflected in a fifteenth-century composition entitled *The Training of Cuchulainn*, in which the hero crosses a Bridge of the Cliff that is: "narrow as a hair, . . . as sharp as a blade edge, and as slippery as an eel's tail" (*Arthurian Tradition and Chrétien de Troyes* [New York: Columbia University Press, 1949], p. 226).

711ff. This description of the knight in love lost in reverie about the loved one and unaware of his surroundings, whose roots lie in the symptoms of love described by Ovid, is repeated in *Perceval* vv. 4200ff (Chrétien de Troyes, *Perceval; or, The Story of the Grail*, trans. Ruth Harwood Cline [Athens: University of Georgia Press, 1985], pp. 115–121).

936ff. It is unclear why Lancelot would prefer to undergo so formidable a chastity test rather than spend the night outdoors. Topsfield notes precedents for Lancelot's behavior (vv. 1216ff) in the Tristan legend and speculates that Chrétien may be satirizing Tristan's wedding night, when his love for Queen Iseut the Fair prevents him from consummating his marriage with Iseut of the White Hands, or the episode in the forest of Morois, when King Mark comes upon the lovers sleeping side by side in their chemises with a sword between them and concludes erroneously that their conduct has been chaste (Topsfield, *Chrétien de Troyes*, pp. 129 and 131).

1098. This is the first of only two references to the queen's name: Guinevere (the second is in v. 3207). Just as the heroine of *Yvain* is unnamed in most manuscripts and referred to as "the lady," the heroine of *Lancelot* is referred to almost exclusively by her social role: "the queen."

1126–1128. MS C reads that Lancelot puts his head (*teste*) through the window (*fenestre*) of the doorway, leading to speculation that the open door may be a Dutch door. Foulet suggests that a better and more probable rhyme with *teste* is *feste*, so that Lancelot is looking up toward the gable or ceiling of the room, in "Appendix I," pp. 289–290.

1213–1215. In the Middle Ages people slept naked, as the maiden does when she realizes Lancelot cannot be seduced and retires to her own room (v. 1268).

1217. The reference is to the monastic rules prescribing silence during the sleeping hours.

1272. The Angevine shilling was the currency of Anjou.

1341. *Yvain* contains a similar allusion: "the wounds of love, by definition, / are worst when nearest their physician" (vv. 1269–1270, p. 38). Ovid uses the idea of love as illness at the end of *Remedies for Love*: "Then there's the matter of food, and I, as befits a physician, / Tell you what you should avoid, what you may safely consume" (Ovid, *The Art of Love*, trans. Rolfe Humphries [Bloomington: Indiana University Press, 1957], p. 205).

1347. The bubbling fountain and stone are reminiscent of the storm-making fountain and stone that feature so prominently in *Yvain*.

1352. Wendelin Foerster notes that Ysoré is a Saracen name that is mentioned on several occasions in medieval literature (Chrétien de Troyes, *Der Karrenritter* [*Lancelot*], ed. Wendelin Foerster [1899; reprint, Amsterdam: Editions RODOPI, 1965], footnote to v. 1364, p. 373).

1452ff. In *Yvain*, a maiden tactfully overlooks a similar moment of weakness of the hero by pretending she has not seen him naked after she cures him of his madness (vv. 2830ff, pp. 84–85).

1461ff. Matilda Tomaryn Bruckner notes that in a similar scene in *Cligés* Alixandre discovers Soredamor's golden hair woven into his shirt ("*Le Chevalier de la Charrette*," in *The Romances of Chrétien de Troyes: A Symposium*, p. 326).

1482. Foerster notes that the Lendit fair was held at St. Denis outside Paris every year beginning June 11 (Chrétien de Troyes, *Der Karrenritter*, footnote to v. 1494, p. 374).

1502. The straight way Lancelot is pursuing has become the narrow way mentioned in Matthew 7:14 "For the gate is narrow and the way is hard, that leads to life, and those who find it are few." The Stony Passageway (vv. 2163ff) is another narrow way.

1570–1573. Chrétien has copied the figure of sailing and arriving in port used by Ovid at the end of *Remedies for Love*: "So, I have finished my work: hang wreaths on the prow of my vessel, / We have come to the port whither my voyage was bound" (Ovid, *The Art of Love*, p. 206).

1719. Enarmes are the straps used to hold a shield.

1749–1750. Elisabeth Schulze-Busacker cites this proverb in *Proverbes et Expressions Proverbiales dans la Littérature Narrative du Moyen Age Français* (Geneva and Paris: Editions Slatkine, 1985), pp. 55 and 273, noting that in the basic form of "*privez mar achate*" it also appears in vv. 8945–8948 of the *Roman d'Enéas*.

1842. This pause to pray in the church is Lancelot's sole and understandable deviation from his resolution to pursue the queen by the straightest, fastest way.

1852ff. The episode of the cemetery, in which Lancelot lifts the marble slab covering the tomb of the liberator of the captives, shows how he is empowered by love with the strength of seven men, confirms the mission for which he is destined, and is a sobering reminder of his own mortality.

1904. MS C reads "where clerks and noblemen are banned." See Foulet, "Appendix I," p. 298.

2008. Yvain assumed an incognito and fought in disguise. Lancelot's refusal to disclose his name may reflect his irritation at the contempt he receives because of the cart or a desire for discretion on his mission into enemy territory. Certainly he has no reason to confide in his seductive hostess or his challenger.

2051–2053. Since the vavasor and his family are prisoners, Lancelot has crossed the border into Gorre.

2134. The Saracens were Muslims connected with the Crusades and the enemies of Christians in those holy wars.

2266. Lancelot is telling time by canonical hours at the beginning of summer. He rises by 5 a.m., at daybreak, and is riding by prime, approximately 6 a.m. Past none is after 3 p.m., but Lancelot refuses to rest until vespers at sundown, which in summer in the British Isles is close to 8 or 9 p.m.

2290. Lancelot has fallen in with an enemy from Gorre. Learning that a liberator has entered Gorre, the Logrian prisoners have rioted. See F. Douglas Kelly, *Sens et Conjointure in the "Chevalier de la Charrette"* (The Hague and Paris: Mouton and Company, 1966), pp. 132–133.

2320ff. This fortress, which captures Lancelot and his party between two sliding doors, is remarkably similar to the episode in *Yvain* where Yvain chases the fatally wounded Esclados the Red back to his castle and is caught between two sliding doors.

2337. In this situation Yvain was given a magic ring of invisibility. Loomis notes in *Arthurian Tradition*, p. 239–240, that "the particular form of the tradition which Chrétien employed in his cursory reference to the ring bestowed on Lancelot by his fairy foster mother is given more fully in the *Vulgate Lancelot*, where we read that the Dame du Lac, on the departure of the young hero from her home, placed on his finger a ring with the assurance that it 'had the power to reveal and make visible all enchantments.'"

2626ff. Topsfield notes that this arrogant knight's offer of an exchange of a life for a service is in the Celtic supernatural tradition, whereas his offer to ferry Lancelot across the river that separates him from the Otherworld is reminiscent of classical boatman Charon ferrying the dead over the River Styx to Hades (*Chrétien de Troyes*, p. 139).

2696. In contrast, Chrétien emphasizes, when Yvain fought with Esclados the Red, "that neither of the knights used force / to try to strike or harm a horse" (*Yvain*, vv. 801–802, p. 25).

2744. This image of the lark and merlin is strikingly similar to the image of the gyrfalcon and crane that Chrétien employs during the battle with Esclados in *Yvain*:

> The knight fled, and the lord Yvain—
> as the gyrfalcon hunts the crane
> he's sighted rising far away,
> and flies so close beside his prey,
> he's certain he's about to clutch her,
> and yet he cannot even touch her—
> was like the falcon. . . .
>
> (*Yvain*, vv. 827–833, pp. 25–26)

2781. A maiden riding on a mule was a traditional messenger from the Otherworld, and there is something supernatural about her mount's speed.

This maiden, fittingly, will prove to be Meleagant's sister.

2820ff. The reference is to Mary as a child of God and the mother of Jesus.

3024. Medieval lances could be sixteen feet long.

3033. These lions or leopards, like the axemen at the Stone Passage, seem to be obstacles that vanish once the hero has proven his courage. Lancelot checks for spells with his fairy ring (v. 3124), but there is no explanation of this terrifying illusion.

3045–3046. MS C reads: "if you don't go back where you went, / much later on you will repent." See Foulet, "Appendix I," pp. 290–291.

3215. Schulze-Busacker cites this variation of the proverb "Qui honor chace honor ataint" on pp. 56 and 288.

3228a, b. Foulet notes that only MSS C and G omit these lines ("Appendix I," p. 291).

3237–3238. MS C reads: "you know full well how much chagrin / this knight will feel if he can't win." See Foulet, "Appendix I," p. 209.

3248. MS C reads "I warn and urge you to make peace." Foulet prefers "I am distressed by your caprice" ("Appendix I," p. 209).

3357. Foerster notes that this precious salve is mentioned in other Arthurian romances and that the three Marys are Mary of Magdala, Mary the mother of James, and Mary Salome, who annointed the body of Jesus after the crucifixion, in Mark 16:1 (Chrétien de Troyes, Der Karrenritter, footnote to v. 3374, p. 389).

3362ff. Under the old custom, the queen would have been defenseless against her abductor. Bademagu, however, has no intention of upholding the old custom, particularly where the wife of a fellow monarch is concerned, and is outraged by his son's rashness.

3481. MS C reads "an aged man." See Foulet, "Appendix I," p. 299.

3485. The school of medicine at Montpellier was noted in the twelfth century.

3660. It is typical of the queen's discretion that she would carefully consider whether the maiden's question had underlying motives before naming the hero for the first time in the manuscript.

3803. The classical tale of the love between Pyramus and Thisbe and their double suicide when each believes the other dead, contained in book 4 of Ovid's Metamorphoses, was well known in the Middle Ages. Frappier notes in Chrétien de Troyes: The Man and His Work (Athens: Ohio University Press, 1982), pp. 172–173, that Chrétien uses the theme in Erec and Cligés and parodies it in Yvain by having Yvain's lion attempt to impale himself on his master's sword when he finds Yvain fallen in a swoon and believes him dead (see Yvain, vv. 3317–3332, p. 99).

3877ff. Clearly, with victory imminent, Lancelot and the queen have conceded a great deal. Meleagant is to proceed to Arthur's court to challenge Lancelot when he sees fit, and one year from the day of this challenge the duel will be refought in the presence of distinguished witnesses. Thus the issue of the queen's freedom will not be permanently resolved until the day of this last battle.

3977–3980. The metaphor of the heart's separating from the body is repeated in v. 4692 and is also used in *Yvain* (vv. 2469–2488), when Yvain leaves his heart behind with Laudine when he departs with Gawain.

4017ff. Kay's description of King Bademagu's arrangements for the queen's protection and his recovery are not inconsistent with the few days the queen and he have stayed at the fortress, but it seems as if they have been there for some time.

4157. The references to malicious, inaccurate, and confusing rumors, also found in vv. 4248–4249 and 4428–4429, recall the rumors about Dido and Aeneas in book 4 of the *Aeneid*, a liaison that resulted in Dido's suicide, and a passage about the palace of Rumor in book 12 of Ovid's *Metamorphoses*, trans. A. D. Melville (Oxford and New York: Oxford University Press, 1986), pp. 275–276: "and rumours everywhere, / Thousands, false mixed with true, roam to and fro."

4197ff. Guyer notes that this love-monologue and others in *Lancelot* and *Yvain* reflect the love-monologues in Ovid's *Metamorphoses*, "in which the speaker gives a natural and complete exposure of the various, disconnected, incoherent thoughts that pass through his mind at a moment of strong emotional excitement. The speaker addresses numerous questions to himself and gives waivering answers which reveal the mental struggle or uncertainty to which the person is subjected. These monologues are preceded or followed by comments on the part of the author so that they appear like little psychological dramas introduced by an author's prologue and followed by his comments" ("Influence of Ovid," p. 128). See Lancelot's love monologue beginning vv. 4318ff.

4201ff. It is possible to explain the queen's refusal to speak to Lancelot in terms of courtly love, in which the lady tests her lover. The queen clearly states that such was not her intention. In a fit of caprice, as a malicious jest, she reestablished the social distance between them as queen and knight in her service and asserted her royal prerogative to speak or not speak to one of her subjects. She also repudiated any suggestion that under the terms of the agreement she had passed from the control of Meleagant to that of Lancelot. The timing of her impulse made her seem most ungrateful, and she is now exceedingly contrite. Later she will explain what role Lancelot's delay in mounting the cart played in her behavior.

4219. Brabanters, from the central Belgian region of Brabant, were mercenary soldiers widely employed in the Middle Ages.

4246 and 4474. Kelly notes that Lancelot's first absence from Bademagu's court, when the people of Gorre capture him and the queen believes him dead, lasts two days (see *Sens et Conjointure*, pp. 132–133).

4387. See *Yvain:*

> Though some hate honor, and love blame,
> and spread their balm on ash and soil,
> put soot in honey, and would spoil
> sweet sugar, mixing it with gall
> Love should not act this way at all!
>
> (vv. 1294–1298, p. 39)

4484–4490. Here the queen gives another explanation for her refusal to speak to Lancelot. It has been noted that, as an obedient wife, she did not hesitate to sacrifice her own pride by throwing herself at Kay's feet when her husband asked it of her.

4520ff. Medieval bedrooms were no havens of privacy. Men and women often shared sleeping quarters in the Middle Ages, and the injured Kay and queen are sharing sleeping quarters with a guard outside. Visitors were also common (see vv. 4746ff).

4544–4545. The figure of night defeating day at twilight and throwing her dark cape over the world is taken directly from book 15 of Ovid's *Metamorphoses* (p. 371):

> twilight drove
> The last late light away. Across the globe
> Darkness had drawn its shadowy canopy.

4737ff. This scene is heavily indebted to the Tristan legend, when a malevolent dwarf sprinkles flour around the royal bed when Tristan is sharing their bedchamber and King Mark has left the couple alone. Seeing the flour, Tristan leaps from bed to bed, leaving no footprints, but betrays himself when drops of blood from a wound on his leg stain the queen's sheets and drip onto the flour. Despite the tenderness of the description of the queen's tryst with Lancelot, the images of Lancelot's stained hands and the queen's besmirched bed hint at Chrétien's views of adultery. The pure white chemise that the queen wears to the tryst and her mortified blush upon the discovery that her seemly pristine sheets are stained are symbolic of her feelings and reputation (v. 4778).

4757ff. Meleagant's comments on the futility of guarding women reflects Ovid's similar observation in book 3, chap. 4, of the *Loves* (*Art of Love*, pp. 73–75).

4944ff. This battle is separate from the battle for the ultimate possession of the queen, which has been postponed for over one year and rescheduled for King Arthur's court. This battle is legal combat, and the issue concerning which both knights, at Lancelot's shrewd insistence, will take oaths on relics is whether Kay was the queen's lover. Since Kay was not, and God will give victory to the man who swears truly, Lancelot will win. This scene again reflects the Tristan legend, when Iseut is tested by King Mark with hot irons about whether Tristan has been her lover. On the way to the trial, Tristan disguises himself as a humble pilgrim and, when the queen slips while crossing a stream, picks her up and assists her to shore. At the trial Iseut takes oath that no man has ever held her in his arms except her husband and the poor pilgrim, picks up the hot iron, and carries it unscathed.

5369. The name of the town has been changed from Noauz (Old French for worst) to Worstede, the old spelling of the Norfolk, England, parish of Worstead, in an attempt to render a complex pun. In vv. 5369–5370, the lines read literally "*l'anprist la dame de Noauz. / De cels qui feront noauz* (challenged by the Lady of Nouaz. / To those who do the worst). In v. 5645 the queen, with her exceptional discretion, believing that she recognizes the lost Lancelot on the field, sends the maiden down with the message "*au noauz.*" Any other knight would interpret her message "to Noauz" as the queen's command to fight on the side of the town of Noauz. "*Au noauz*" can also mean "Do your worst," but only Lancelot would interpret her command that way. To test Lancelot's obedience a final time, the queen repeats "*au noauz*" in v. 5842 "*qu'au noauz' le reface ancor*" and then gives him the command "*au mieux,*" or "do your best."

5389ff. Repeating the rash boon motif, King Arthur again promises to grant an unknown favor. The queen's feelings can be imagined.

5536ff. The herald has been gambling away his clothing in the tavern.

5563. Schulze-Busacker cites this proverb on pp. 265–266. William A. Nitze notes that Margery Ellis identified this expression in *A Catalogue of the Proverbs of Chrétien de Troyes*, a Master's dissertation accepted by the University of Chicago in 1927 (Nitze, " 'Or est venuz qui aunera': A Medieval Dictum," *Modern Language Notes* 56, no. 6 [June 1941]: 405–409). The measure to be taken is for a grave, and the one to take the measure is Death. Gaston Paris based his not-widely accepted theory that Chrétien may have been a herald on this passage.

5622. Kelly notes that Lancelot "fights alone as well as twenty men and four times better than the son of the King of Ireland, the best knight in the tournament after him" (*Sens et Conjointure,* p. 41).

5770. Knights vowed to a crusade were exempt from participation in tournaments. Ménard relates that in 1177 the Count of Champagne took the cross and later in 1179 led a French expedition to the Holy Land ("Note sur la date," p. 121).

6074. Mario Roques notes that the giant might be Dinabuc, who terrorized Mont-Saint-Michel by sinking ships with huge stones and killing and devouring travelers (Chrétien de Troyes, *Le Chevalier de la Charrette* [Paris: ·Champion, 1970], p. 225). Arthur's slaying of this giant is mentioned by Geoffrey of Monmouth and Wace (Geoffrey of Monmouth, *History of the Kings of Britain,* book 10, chap. 3, pp. 237–238).

6132. At approximately this point, when the steward returned home and Meleagant had the tower built, immured Lancelot, and went to court, Chrétien turned *Lancelot* over to Godefroy de Leigny with an outline.

6200. The importance of this battle would be clearer if Godefroy de Leigny had mentioned that it is the battle to determine whether the queen will remain with Arthur or will become Meleagant's prisoner forever. Since Meleagant's motives seem more vainglorious than lustful, he is willing to accept as a substitute Gawain, the finest knight against whom Lancelot, Yvain, and Perceval measure themselves.

6393ff. Meleagant's sister's random search for Lancelot resembles the younger daughter of the Lord of the Black Thorn's search for Yvain:

> the maid
> began her quest and rode about
> in many different lands without
> a word of news of him.
> (*Yvain,* vv. 4596ff, p. 136)

6437. This is the first of several references to the classical goddess Fortuna, who determines the fates of humans with the turns of her wheel.

6621. Footnote 51 in Kelly, *Sens et Conjointure,* p. 146: Gaston Paris, "Etudes," *Romania* 12: 482, n. 2, and Wendelin Foerster, in Chrétien's *Der Karrenritter,* p. LXXXV, "wonder that Bademagu's daughter could find a pick-axe in the wilderness. Foerster's suggestion is perfectly feasible: the workers left it behind when they completed the tower."

6679ff. Lancelot and Meleagant's young sister address one another so tenderly that Shirt speculated that she might have replaced Guinevere in his affections ("Godefroy de Lagny et la composition de la Charrette," *Romania* 96 [1975]: 39–52). Nonetheless, the observation that she cared for Lancelot as tenderly as if he were her father (v. 6668) seems intended to reflect both the nature of their relationship and the considerable difference in their ages. In a similar scene of exuberant gratitude, Yvain kisses Lunette, calls her "my sweet friend," and vows her everlasting service when she arranges his reconciliation with his wife (*Yvain*, vv. 6389ff, p. 189).

6780. Bucephalus was the war horse of Alexander the Great.

6956–6957. This French version of "It is too late to lock the barn door after the horse has been stolen" was proverbial in the twelfth century. Schulze-Busacker cites it together with subsequent works in which it appears (*Proverbes et Expressions Proverbiales*, p. 184).

6983ff. Bruckner notes that "the combat takes place in a typical setting for love: a *locus amoenus* complete with fresh grass, ancient sycamore and clear fountain" ("*Le Chevalier de la Charrette*," p. 329).

7102. Chrétien's decision to turn the remainder of the romance over to Godefroy de Leigny when Lancelot was walled in the tower, has serious implications for the ending. It can be believed that Godefroy de Leigny followed Chrétien's outline scrupulously: Meleagant returns to court to issue his challenge, and the year begins to run its course. Lancelot escapes Meleagant's attempt to starve him in the tower, arrives at court at the last moment for the final battle, and beheads Meleagant. In a setting for love that has been turned into a battleground the queen plans a second tryst. But Godefroy's handling of the ending fails to emphasize that this last battle is for the queen, and if Meleagant wins she will become his prisoner forever and be lost to both Arthur and Lancelot. When Meleagant issues his challenge before Arthur, he does not mention the queen but simply refers to the terms that were arranged. Lancelot's lengthy lament in the tower does not contain one word of concern about the queen's fate or his personal loss if he fails to appear at court, whereas Chrétien presents Yvain as acutely aware of the time. In the last battle, the focus is entirely on Lancelot and Meleagant, and no mention is made of the liberation of the queen. The romance ends with jubilation about a beheading, and the significance of the battle is lost. The tournament episode, which may have been written and inserted after Godefroy wrote this conclusion, counterbalances but does not entirely mitigate its flaws.

BIBLIOGRAPHY

This bibliography contains only the references used in the preparation of this translation. The reader is referred to Douglas Kelly's *Chrétien de Troyes, An Analytic Bibliography* (London: Grant and Cutler, 1977) for a comprehensive survey of the literature on the works of Chrétien. Other bibliographies compiled annually include the *Bibliographical Bulletin of the International Arthurian Society* and the *Bibliography* of the Modern Language Association.

Andreas Capellanus. *The Art of Courtly Love.* Translated by John Jay Parry, and edited by Frederick W. Locke. New York: Frederick Ungar Publishing Co., 1957.

The Arthurian Encyclopedia. Edited by Norris J. Lacy. New York and London: Garland Publishing, 1986.

Ashe, Geoffrey. *King Arthur's Avalon: The Story of Glastonbury.* Glasgow: William Collins Sons and Co., Fontana Books, 1980.

Barber, Richard. *King Arthur, Hero and Legend.* Woodbridge, Suffolk: Boydell Press, 1986. First published in 1961 as *Arthur of Albion.* Second edition revised and extended in 1973 as *King Arthur in Legend and History.* Third edition, revised and extended, 1986.

Benton, John F. "The Court of Champagne as a Literary Center." *Speculum* 36, no. 4 (October 1961): 551–591.

Bogin, Meg. *The Women Troubadours.* New York and London: W. W. Norton and Company, 1980.

Brooke, Christopher. "Geoffrey of Monmouth as a Historian." In *Church and Government in the Middle Ages,* edited by C. Brooke et al., pp. 77–91. Cambridge: Cambridge University Press, 1976.

Bruckner, Matilda Tomaryn. "*Le Chevalier de la Charrette.*" In *The Romances of Chrétien de Troyes: A Symposium,* edited by Douglas Kelly, pp. 132–181 and notes. Lexington, Ky.: French Forum Publishers, 1985.

———. "An Interpreter's Dilemma: Why Are There So Many Interpretations of Chrétien's *Chevalier de la Charrette?*" *Romance Philology* 40 (1986–1987): 159–180.

Chrétien de Troyes. *Arthurian Romances.* Translated by W. Wistar Comfort. Everyman's Library, no. 98. London: J. M. Dent and Sons, 1914.

———. *Arthurian Romances.* Translated by D. D. R. Owen. Everyman's Library, no. 1698. London: J. M. Dent and Sons, 1987.

————. *Le Chevalier de la Charrette (Lancelot)*. Translated by Jean Frappier. Paris: Champion, 1967.

————. *Le Chevalier de la Charrette*. Edited by Mario Roques. Les classiques français du moyen âge. Paris: Champion, 1970.

————. *Cligés*. Edited by Alexandre Micha. Paris: Champion, 1957.

————. *Der Karrenritter (Lancelot) and Das Wilhelmsleben (Guillaume d'Angleterre)*. Edited by Wendelin Foerster. 1899. Reprint. Amsterdam: Editions RODOPI, 1965.

————. *Lancelot; or, The Knight of the Cart*. Edited and translated by William W. Kibler. New York and London: Garland Publishing, 1981.

————. *Lancelot: The Knight of the Cart*. Translated by Deborah Webster Rogers, with an introduction by W. T. H. Jackson. New York: Columbia University Press, 1984.

————. *Perceval; or, The Story of the Grail*. Translated by Ruth Harwood Cline. Athens: University of Georgia Press, 1985.

————. *Yvain; or, The Knight with the Lion*. Translated by Ruth Harwood Cline. Athens: University of Georgia Press, 1975.

Cross, Tom Peete, and William A. Nitze. *Lancelot and Guinevere: A Study on the Origins of Courtly Love*, pp. 20–66. Chicago: University of Chicago Press, 1930.

Dufournet, Jean. "Bibliographie. Chrétien de Troyes: *Le Chevalier de la Charrette*." *Le Moyen Age* 70 (1968): 503–523.

Dumville, David N. " 'Nennius' and the '*Historia Brittonum*.' " *Studia Celtae* 10–11 (1975–1976): 78–95.

Flint, Valerie I. J. "The *Historia Regum Britanniae* of Geoffrey of Monmouth: Parody and Its Purpose, a Suggestion." *Speculum* 54 (July 1979): 447–468.

Fotitch, Tatania. *The Narrative Tenses in Chrétien de Troyes*. Washington, D.C.: Catholic University of America Press, 1950.

Foulet, Alfred. "Appendix I: On Editing Chrétien's *Lancelot*." In *The Romances of Chrétien de Troyes: A Symposium*. Edited by Douglas Kelly, pp. 287–309. Lexington, Ky.: French Forum Publishers, 1985.

Fowler, David C. "L'amour dans le *Lancelot* de Chrétien." *Romania* 91 (1970): 378–391.

————. "Love in Chrétien's *Lancelot*." *Romanic Review* 63 (1972): 5–14.

Frappier, Jean. *Chrétien de Troyes*. Paris: Hatier, 1968.

————. *Chrétien de Troyes: The Man and His Work*. English translation of 1968 edition by Raymond J. Cormier. Athens: Ohio University Press, 1982.

————. "Le motif du don contraignant dans la littérature du moyen âge." *Travaux de linguistique et de littérature* 7 (1969): 7–46. Reprinted in *Amour Courtois et Table Ronde*, pp. 225–264. Geneva: Droz, 1973.

——— . "Le Prologue du *Chevalier de la Charrette* et son interprétation." *Romania* 93 (1972): 337–379.

Geoffrey of Monmouth. *The History of the Kings of Britain*. Translated by Lewis Thorpe. 1966. Reprint. Harmondsworth, Middlesex: Penguin Books, 1979.

Grigsby, John L. "Narrative Voices in Chrétien de Troyes: A Prolegomenon to Dissection." *Romance Philology* 32 (1979): 261–273.

Guyer, Foster E. "The Influence of Ovid on Chrétien de Troyes." *Romanic Review* 12, no. 2–3 (1921): 126–131, 216–232.

Holmes, Urban T., Jr. *Chrétien de Troyes*. New York: Twayne Publishers, 1970.

Hult, David F. "Lancelot's Two Steps: A Problem in Textual Criticism." *Speculum* 61 (1986): 836–858.

Jackson, W. T. H. "The *De Amore* of Andreas Capellanus and the Practice of Love at Court." *Romanic Review* 49 (1958): 243–251.

Jones, Thomas. "The Early Evolution of the Legend of Arthur." *Nottingham Medieval Studies* 8 (1964): 3–21.

Kelly, Amy. *Eleanor of Aquitaine and the Four Kings*. New York: Random House, Vintage Books, 1950.

Kelly, F. Douglas. *Sens et Conjointure in the "Chevalier de la Charrette,"* pp. 21–30, 38–69, 102–149, 192–193, 206–229. The Hague and Paris: Mouton and Company, 1966.

Kibler, William W. "*Le Chevalier de la Charrette* de Mario Roques: Corrections." *Romania* 105 (1984): 558–564.

——— . *An Introduction to Old French*. New York: Modern Language Association of America, 1984.

Lacy, Norris J. *The Craft of Chrétien de Troyes: An Essay on Narrative Art*. Davis Medieval Texts and Studies, vol. 3. Leiden: E. J. Brill, 1980.

——— . "Spacial Form in Medieval Romance." *French Studies* 51 (1974): 160–169.

Laurie, Helen C. R. "*Enéas* and the *Lancelot* of Chrétien de Troyes." *Medium Aevum* 37, no. 2 (1968): 142–156.

Liebermann, F. "Nennius: The Author of the *Historia Brittonum*." In *Essays in Medieval History Presented to T. F. Font,* edited by A. G. Little and F. M. Pewicke, pp. 25–44. Manchester: Manchester University Press, 1925.

Loomis, Roger Sherman. *Arthurian Tradition and Chrétien de Troyes*. New York: Columbia University Press, 1949.

Luttrell, Claude A. *The Creation of the First Arthurian Romance: A Quest*. London: Edward Arnold, 1974.

McCash, June Hall Martin. "Marie de Champagne and Eleanor of Aquitaine: A Relationship Reexamined." *Speculum* 54 (October 1979): 698–711.

Meade, Marion. *Eleanor of Aquitaine: A Biography.* New York: Hawthorn/ Dutton, 1977.

Ménard, Philippe. "Note sur la date du *Chevalier de la Charrette.*" *Romania* 92 (1974): 118–26.

––––––. "Un terme de jeu dans le *Chevalier de la Charrette:* le mot san." *Romania* 91 (1970): 400–405.

Nitze, William A. " 'Or est venuz qui aunera': A Medieval Dictum." *Modern Language Notes* 56, no. 6 (June 1941): 405–409.

––––––. *Perceval and the Holy Grail.* University of California Publications in Modern Theology, vol. 28, no. 5. Berkeley and Los Angeles: University of California Press, 1949.

Noble, Peter S. *Love and Marriage in Chrétien de Troyes.* Cardiff: University of Wales Press, 1982.

Nykl, Alois Richard. *Hispano-Arab Poetry and Its Relations with the Old Provençal Troubadours.* Baltimore: J. H. Furst Company, 1946.

Ollier, Marie-Louise. "The Author in the Text: The Prologues of Chrétien de Troyes." *French Studies* 51 (1974): 26–41.

Ovid. *The Art of Love.* Translated by Rolfe Humphries. Bloomington: Indiana University Press, 1957.

––––––. *The Metamorphoses.* Translated by A. D. Melville. Oxford and New York: Oxford University Press, 1986.

Paden, William D., Jr. "The Troubadour's Lady: Her Marital Status and Social Rank." *Studies in Philology* 72 (1975): 28–50.

La Portée Arturienne du Roman de Brut. Edited by I. D. O. Arnold and M. M. Pelan. Paris: Klincksieck, 1962.

Rahilly, Leonard J. "Le manuscrit Garrett 125 du *Chevalier de la Charrette* et du *Chevalier au Lion:* un nouveau manuscrit." *Romania* 94 (1973): 407–410.

––––––. "La tradition manuscrite du *Chevalier de la Charrette* et le manuscrit Garrett 125." *Romania* 95 (1974): 395–413.

Robertson, D. W., Jr. "Some Medieval Literary Terminology with Special Reference to Chrétien de Troyes." *Studies in Philology* 48 (1951): 669–692.

The Romance of Arthur. Edited by James J. Wilhelm and Laila Zamuelis Gross. New York and London: Garland Publishing, 1984.

The Romance of Arthur II. Edited by James J. Wilhelm. New York and London: Garland Publishing, 1986.

The Romances of Chrétien de Troyes: A Symposium. Edited by Douglas Kelly. Lexington, Ky.: French Forum Publishers, 1985.

Schulze-Busacker, Elisabeth. *Proverbes et Expressions Proverbiales dans la Littéra-*

ture Narrative du Moyen Age Français. Geneva and Paris: Editions Slatkine, 1985.

Shirt, David J. "Chrétien's *Charrette* and Its Critics, 1964–74." *Modern Language Review* 73 (1978): 38–50.

――――. "Chrétien de Troyes et une coutume anglaise." *Romania* 94 (1973): 178–195.

――――. "Godefroy de Lagny et la composition de la *Charrette*." *Romania* 96 (1975): 27–52.

――――. "How Much of the Lion Can We Put Before the Cart?" *French Studies* 31 (1977): 1–17.

――――. "*Le Chevalier de la Charrette:* A World Upside Down?" *Modern Language Review* 76 (1981): 811–822.

Terry, Patricia. *Lays of Courtly Love*. New York: Doubleday and Company, Anchor Books, 1963.

Topsfield, L. T. *Chrétien de Troyes: A Study of the Arthurian Romances*, pp. 1–20, 105–174. Cambridge and New York: Cambridge University Press, 1981.

Uitti, Karl D. "Autant en Emporte Li Funs: Remarques sur le Prologue du *Chevalier de la Charrette* de Chrétien de Troyes." *Romania* 105 (1984): 270–291.

Breinigsville, PA USA
01 March 2010

233351BV00001B/2/P